TECHNICAL
REPORT

Value-Added Assessment in Practice

Lessons from the Pennsylvania
Value-Added Assessment System
Pilot Project

Daniel F. McCaffrey, Laura S. Hamilton

Supported by the Carnegie Corporation of New York,
the Ewing Marion Kauffman Foundation, the National Education Association,
and the Pennsylvania State Education Association

RAND EDUCATION

The research described in this report was conducted within RAND Education, a division of the RAND Corporation. It was funded by the Carnegie Corporation of New York, the Ewing Marion Kauffman Foundation, the National Education Association, and the Pennsylvania State Education Association. Additional funding came from the Connecticut Education Association, Education Minnesota, and the Ohio Education Association.

Library of Congress Cataloging-in-Publication Data

McCaffrey, Daniel F.
    Value-added assessment in practice : lessons from the Pennsylvania Value-Added Assessment System pilot project / Daniel F. McCaffrey, Laura S. Hamilton.
        p. cm.
    Includes bibliographical references.
    ISBN 978-0-8330-4236-1 (pbk. : alk. paper)
    1. Educational tests and measurements—Pennsylvania. 2. Educational accountability—United States. 3. Educational indicators—United States. I. Hamilton, Laura S. II. Title.

LB3052.P46M33 2007
371.26'2—dc22

                                                                                    2007038195

The RAND Corporation is a nonprofit research organization providing objective analysis and effective solutions that address the challenges facing the public and private sectors around the world. RAND's publications do not necessarily reflect the opinions of its research clients and sponsors.

RAND® is a registered trademark.

Published 2007 by the RAND Corporation
1776 Main Street, P.O. Box 2138, Santa Monica, CA 90407-2138
1200 South Hayes Street, Arlington, VA 22202-5050
4570 Fifth Avenue, Suite 600, Pittsburgh, PA 15213-2665
RAND URL: http://www.rand.org/
To order RAND documents or to obtain additional information, contact
Distribution Services: Telephone: (310) 451-7002;
Fax: (310) 451-6915; Email: order@rand.org

Preface

In response to the test-based accountability systems that have been adopted by states, school and district staff are increasingly using student achievement data to make decisions about curriculum and instruction. Many states and districts in the United States have begun providing staff with information from value-added assessment systems. In this context, *value-added assessment* refers to a collection of statistical techniques designed in part to use longitudinal student test scores to provide measures on the effectiveness of individual schools and teachers. This study examines a value-added assessment program in one state, Pennsylvania, with a focus on examining the effects of the program on student achievement and on the ways it has been implemented at the district, school, and classroom levels.

This research was conducted within RAND Education and reflects RAND Education's mission to bring accurate data and careful, objective analysis to the national debate on education policy. This study is part of a larger body of RAND Education work addressing value-added modeling, assessment, and accountability. The study was funded by the Carnegie Corporation of New York, the Ewing Marion Kauffman Foundation, the National Education Association, and the Pennsylvania State Education Association. Additional funding came from the Connecticut Education Association, Education Minnesota, and the Ohio Education Association. Any opinions, findings, and conclusions or recommendations expressed in this material are those of the authors and do not necessarily reflect the views of these organizations.

The principal author of this work may be contacted by email at Daniel_McCaffrey@rand.org or by phone at 310-393-0411, x4919. For more information on RAND Education, contact the Director, Susan Bodilly. She can be reached by email at Susan_Bodilly@rand.org, by phone at 703-413-1100, x5377, or by mail at the RAND Corporation, 1200 South Hayes St., Arlington, VA 22202-5050. More information about RAND is available at http://www.rand.org

Contents

Figures

Tables

Summary

Introduction

The use of student achievement data for decisionmaking is currently a focus of school and district reform efforts across the United States. Emphasis on data has grown as result of an increasing emphasis on using test scores to evaluate school performance, a use that is central to the No Child Left Behind[1] (NCLB) accountability provisions. Data use has also been facilitated by improved data systems and analysis tools. This technology has contributed to the growing use of value-added assessment (VAA) systems[2]—collections of complex statistical techniques that use multiple years of test-score data on students to try to estimate the causal effects of individual schools or teachers on student learning. The Tennessee Value-Added Assessment System (TVAAS) is the most widely known application of VAA in the United States, and efforts to extend or replicate this model are currently under way in other states and school districts.

VAA can be used to support external accountability and monitoring of school performance. It can also be used as a tool for promoting school improvement by providing data to help school personnel make decisions. To date, most VAA programs have emphasized the latter use. In these contexts, VAA is intended to contribute to better decisions about educational practice, which in turn should promote improved student achievement. This study is designed to evaluate the extent to which a VAA system achieves the goals of improving practice and student outcomes. It examines one recently adopted VAA system—the Pennsylvania Value-Added Assessment System, or PVAAS. Pennsylvania rolled out its system in four waves, which resulted in a quasi-experimental condition, with a subset of the school districts participating in PVAAS and a subset of possible comparison districts not in the program. This report describes an investigation of PVAAS that explores three related questions:

---

[1] Signed into law January 8, 2002, No Child Left Behind (NCLB) is the latest revision of the 1965 Elementary and Secondary Education Act. It establishes high learning standards for all students, including requirements that all students be proficient in reading and mathematics by 2013–2014. Among other provisions, it also requires that all students be tested against state standards in grades 3 to 8 and one high school grade in reading and mathematics and three times in their school career in science. The law mandates that schools be assessed on the basis of student test scores on their Adequate Yearly Progress toward the 2014 goals.

[2] Value-added assessment is sometimes referred to as value-added analysis, value-added modeling, or growth modeling. Because the Pennsylvania pilot program studied in this report is called the Pennsylvania Value-Added Assessment System, for consistency of terminology within the report, we use the term *value-added assessment* to refer to the value-added information created from test-score data and provided to schools.

1. What is the effect on student achievement of providing districts with information from a VAA system?
2. How does the use of data by educators whose districts participate in a VAA system differ from that of educators from nonparticipating districts?
3. How do educators respond to the VAA information they receive?

The first question is the causal question of primary interest. The second and third questions are intended to clarify the mechanisms through which provision of VAA information might affect practice and, ultimately, student achievement.

Methods

Because the pilot districts were not randomly chosen, the study matched the first two cohorts of PVAAS pilot districts to comparison districts by finding a sample with the smallest average distance between pilot and comparison districts in terms of demographic and historic test scores using an optimization algorithm. Overall, the matches for both cohorts were very similar in terms of over 100 variables describing the district's student demographics and historic achievement, district financing, and the populations living in each district as measured by the 2000 Census.

The effects of PVAAS on student achievement on the state's accountability test were measured by differences between students in the pilot and matched comparison districts. Several analyses test for effects, including models based on district aggregates, nonparametric methods, and mixed models with and without controls for student- and district-level variables.

The study surveyed all superintendents, 411 principals, and 2,379 teachers from the 93 study districts (47 PVAAS and 46 matched comparison districts) during the second half of the 2005–2006 school year. Over 85 percent of superintendents (or their designees), 58 percent of principals, and 44 percent of teachers responded to the survey. Responses from all educators are weighted by the inverse of the response probability, to account for differential nonresponse rates. Because many responding principals and teachers had little contact with PVAAS, we focus on educators who are "engaged" in the program (principals who saw the PVAAS reports and knew their school was participating in the program, or teachers who had heard of PVAAS and knew their school was participating in the pilot). We developed weights for comparison principals and teachers to match them to the engaged PVAAS samples on school and district variables.

Survey questions probed educators about their attitudes toward state tests and the state accountability system. They also asked educators about their use of test data for decisions and their training in the analysis and use of data. Items specifically for the educators in the pilot districts asked about PVAAS training, use of PVAAS data, and knowledge of the PVAAS methods. All survey instruments were reviewed by educators and state officials and were revised in response to their comments.

Study Limitations

A primary limitation of this study is the small number of pilot districts available for the study, which placed constraints on matching and limited our power for comparing pilot and comparison districts. Another limitation is the possibility that PVAAS and comparison districts differed on unobserved variables. PVAAS districts needed to have district-wide testing, and we are unable to use such data when selecting comparison districts. For comparing student outcomes, matching on the extensive historical test-score data is likely to mitigate bias from such unobserved differences. However, educators in PVAAS districts tend to report greater emphasis on testing than their counterparts in comparison districts, and this is consistent with bias to preexisting difference in testing experiences. Also the study lacked longitudinal data on individual students. Although we matched on school-level test score trajectories, it is possible that individual students' achievement growth differed in pilot and comparison districts, and any such differences could not be controlled for by our matching procedure.

Low response rates among principals and teachers also limit our sample sizes and could introduce bias. Nonresponse weighting removes differences between respondents and nonrespondents on a large number of factors, but unobserved differences might remain after weighting. Another potential for bias from unobserved differences exist in the comparisons of engaged PVAAS principals and teachers and the educators from the comparison group. Although the engaged and comparison groups are similar on observed school and district variables, we lacked data on individual attributes, such as training or familiarity with data analysis, and remaining differences on such factors could bias comparisons. Finally, we studied the PVAAS districts in their initial years of the program participation. This design may not have provided enough time for school and district staff to learn to use the data effectively. Moreover, even if the use of PVAAS data is highly effective for students in schools and districts that are exposed to it over time, exposure might not have been sufficient in the PVAAS pilot.

Findings

PVAAS Did Not Affect Student Achievement

There were no statistically significant differences in student achievement between PVAAS pilot districts and matched comparison districts. In all comparisons across both cohorts, the differences in means between the pilot and comparison districts were generally small relative to the standard deviations in the scores, ranging from less than 1 percent to about 15 percent of a standard deviation. Moreover, for Cohort 2 districts, the differences between the scores for the PVAAS and comparison districts in the year before districts received their PVAAS reports were similar in direction and magnitude to the differences observed during the next two years. The results provide no evidence that participation in PVAAS affected student achievement.

District Administrators' Use of Achievement Data for Decisionmaking Was Similar in PVAAS and Comparison Districts

Analyses of the survey data suggest possible reasons for the lack of effects on achievement. At all three levels of the education system—district administrators, school principals, and classroom teachers—there was little evidence that use of achievement data differed between PVAAS and non-PVAAS districts, or that PVAAS information was being used in significant ways. Among district administrators, PVAAS participants were slightly more likely than nonparticipants to report that various forms of achievement data were useful for decisionmaking, but the only type of data for which the groups differed significantly was growth data. Both groups reported using data for a number of different decisions. Administrators in PVAAS districts were slightly more likely to support data analysis in their districts through provision of staff and professional development, though the differences were not statistically significant. Although both groups reported receiving technical assistance with data analysis fairly rarely, among those who did receive it, PVAAS administrators were significantly more likely to rate it as useful. In addition, they were less likely than nonparticipants to view insufficient technology or lack of information about growth in achievement as hindrances to their ability to use data effectively.

District Administrators' Opinions of PVAAS Were Positive, But Use Was Limited

The opinions of PVAAS among administrators from pilot districts are generally favorable. A large majority (80 percent) stated that PVAAS provides accurate information about how the district is improving student achievement, compared with fewer than half who endorsed a similar statement about the Adequate Yearly Progress (AYP) measure. Similarly large majorities reported that it helps with communications with parents and helps school staff to see their efforts pay off. Slightly more than half reported that at least some schools in their districts look better with the PVAAS measure than they do using AYP status, so there is clearly a recognition that these sources of information can lead to different conclusions schools' performance. Three-quarters of administrators reported that PVAAS eliminates excuses for poor performance because it measures growth.

Despite their favorable opinions, administrators' use of PVAAS is not as widespread as might be expected. Ninety percent of administrators reported seeing the actual PVAAS reports, and about 70 percent of administrators reported giving teachers in their districts access to these reports. When asked about specific uses of PVAAS information, only a minority of administrators answered that they use PVAAS moderately or extensively in each case. PVAAS is most widely used for making curricular and professional development decisions and improvement planning. For these activities, administrators in about half the districts reported moderate or extensive use. For all decisions, reported use of PVAAS is substantially lower than for other data sources, particularly PSSA scores.

Many Principals Had Limited Experiences with PVAAS and Made Minimal Use of the Information It Provided

The most significant finding from the analysis of principal survey results is that 28 percent of principals in PVAAS districts do not know that their school is participating in the program, and another 14 percent have never seen the PVAAS reports. Because effects of PVAAS on principals' practices are likely to occur only if principals are knowledgeable of the program and the information it provides, we limited subsequent analyses to the 58 percent of principals who are engaged in PVAAS (i.e., they knew their schools were participating and had seen the reports).

Among principals engaged in PVAAS, attitudes about PVAAS are generally positive, though use of the information is somewhat limited. Nearly 80 percent feel PVAAS provides an accurate indication of how well their schools are improving achievement. A majority (60 percent) reported making changes to their leadership or school improvement plan based on PVAAS, and 56 responded that PVAAS helps motivate them. However, smaller percentages agreed or strongly agreed that PVAAS was discussed frequently at staff planning meeting (33 percent), caused the school to focus more on low-performing or high performing students (43 percent and 33 percent, respectively), was used to identify students at risk of not meeting the standards (42 percent), or helped with communications with parents (27 percent). A comparison with these principals' reports of use of other state and district test-score data indicates that PVAAS is not being used as extensively as these other data sources. In general, principals' reports are consistent with those from district administrators, but principals are slightly less enthusiastic and reported slightly lower levels of understanding of the information compared with district administrators.

There Are Few Differences Between PVAAS and Comparison Principals

Principals' responses are important to understand because, as the instructional leaders of their schools, principals play an important role in ensuring that school staff use PVAAS information in ways that will contribute to improved student achievement. Our analyses compared the 58 percent of pilot principals who were engaged in PVAAS to the sample of comparison school principals that was weighted to match to the characteristics of the engaged principals' schools.

The survey results suggest a low level of engagement with PVAAS on the part of many principals, and few differences in the actions taken by principals participating in the PVAAS pilot program and their counterparts from nonparticipating schools. There were a few differences between the groups in their access to resources for data use: PVAAS principals were more likely than comparison principals to receive training on how to use test-score data for instructional planning and to receive information on data systems or guidance on selecting these systems. Other resources, such as professional development to help principals analyze data or to meet the needs of low-achieving students, were available to similar percentages of principals in both groups. Principals' perceptions of the factors that hindered their ability to use data were similar, with one exception: Over half of the comparison group principals (57 percent) reported that lack of data on student growth was a hindrance, but only 27 percent of the engaged pilot principals reported the same. This difference was much larger than any other differences between the groups on these items, and it parallels the finding for district administrators.

Teachers Are Not Engaged with PVAAS

To the extent that providing PVAAS information leads to improved student achievement, it is likely that this effect occurs in large part as a result of actions taken by teachers. As with principals, the most important finding from the teacher surveys is a relatively low level of engagement. Fewer than half of the surveyed teachers in PVAAS pilot districts reported that they had heard of PVAAS, and among those who had heard of the program, only half were aware of their schools' involvement in it. This lack of widespread knowledge of the program on the part of teachers provides one likely explanation for the lack of achievement differences between pilot and comparison districts.

Among the PVAAS teachers who were aware of the program and their school's involvement in it, there was wide variation in use of the information and level of understanding of it. For example, only a small minority understood that PVAAS was not part of schools' AYP calculations, and only about half expressed confidence in their understanding of the meaning of "a school effect" or in their ability to use PVAAS to guide their instruction. Comparisons of attitudes and practices related to data use suggest few differences between these PVAAS teachers and their counterparts in nonparticipating schools, though there is some evidence that the PVAAS teachers are more engaged with data use and test preparation in general.

Conclusions

This study was designed to shed light on the utility of a value-added assessment system for promoting educational improvement. The lack of effects of the program on student achievement are not surprising, given the limited implementation of the pilot program at the district, school, and classroom levels and the relatively short period of time during which the program was in place. The primary finding from the surveys is a lack of use, and in many cases even awareness, of PVAAS among educators—particularly teachers, the group most directly responsible for promoting student learning. This limited use is consistent with findings from research on other VAA systems, both in the United States and in England, where such systems have been in place for some time. The growing body of literature on VAA implementation suggests that providing educators with assistance to help them understand and use the data is likely to be one of the primary challenges associated with adopting such systems. In particular, the survey results from this study indicate a need for training focused on how to make use of the data rather than simply how to interpret it. Pennsylvania has revised its training materials since this study was conducted and is taking steps to improve the support provided to assist educators in their efforts to use the data for improving curriculum and instruction. These actions might increase the likelihood that PVAAS will contribute to more-effective decisionmaking, which in turn might eventually influence student outcomes.

The findings also suggest that one of the challenges to using PVAAS is the need for teachers and administrators to respond to accountability pressures imposed by NCLB. Although advocates of VAA systems often argue that the information these systems provide can be helpful for meeting NCLB goals, the immediate pressure to worry about whether students are proficient may cause educators to focus more of their attention on the state test scores and proficiency levels rather than on the PVAAS information. Combined with the results of other studies on VAA systems, the results of this study could be cautiously interpreted as suggesting that the lack of accountability attached to PVAAS might contribute to the relatively low use. The use of students' growth in achievement as the basis of accountability is increasing in some places, particularly through pay-for-performance measures, such as those promoted by the federal government's Teacher Incentive Fund and through the U.S. Department of Education's Growth Model Pilot program, which allows states to incorporate growth data into their AYP calculations. More generally, achievement growth data are becoming more widely available as a result of improved state and district data systems and analysis tools, and data-driven decisionmaking is being emphasized in many school and district reform efforts. Together, these trends are likely to increase educators' awareness of and interest in using VAA data.

Acknowledgments

This report benefited greatly from the assistance of many people. Elizabeth Stuart of Johns Hopkins University and Donald Rubin of Harvard University designed and led the matching of districts. Jake Dembosky oversaw the fielding of the survey. Sarah Hooper conducted follow-up surveys of district and school administrators. Natalie Swensson provided administrative support for the survey, and Robert Hickam provided expert administrative and editorial support throughout the project. Francis McCaffrey cajoled superintendents and principals into completing the surveys.

Kristen Lewald of Intermediate Unit 13 provided unique insights into PVAAS and offered valuable comments on the survey instruments and drafts of the report. June Rivers of SAS also provide valuable suggestions for the survey instruments. Shula Nedley and Milad Elhadri of the Pennsylvania Department of Education provided us with the student test-score data used in the study. David Wazeter and Harris Zwerling of the Pennsylvania State Education Association offered useful commentary on the survey instruments and draft reports. They also helped with developing the sampling frame for teachers. Darrel Drury of the National Education Association provided insightful comments on the survey instruments and draft reports.

Steve Iovino of the Warwick School District, LaVerne Anthony, Sally Rifugiato, and Marla Pelkofer of Pittsburgh Public Schools, and Kim Schlemmer and Debbie Bender of the Ephrata Area School District piloted tested the survey instruments and gave us useful information that significantly improved the final surveys.

Finally, we thank John Pane and Cathy Stasz of RAND and Marsha Lewis of Ohio University for their timely, thorough, and very thoughtful reviews of the report. Their comments and constructive criticism substantially improved the final report.

Despite the cooperation, support, and guidance of these individuals, any errors in this report remain our own.

Abbreviations

AUN   administrative unit number

AYP   Adequate Yearly Progress

DIBELS   Dynamic Indicators of Basic Early Literacy Skills

DRA   Developmental Reading Assessment

ELL   English language learner

GBM   generalized boosting methods

NCE   normal curve equivalent

NCLB   No Child Left Behind Act of 2001

NDD   no detectable difference

PDE   Pennsylvania Department of Education

PSEA   Pennsylvania State Education Association

PSSA   Pennsylvania System of School Assessment

PVAAS   Pennsylvania Value-Added Assessment System

SOAR   School's Online Achievement Results

TANF   Temporary Assistance for Needy Families

TVAAS   Tennessee Value-Added Assessment System

VAA   value-added assessment

CHAPTER ONE

Introduction

The use of standardized test scores to inform and motivate instructional change is now a cornerstone of education policy in the United States. Systems that rely on test scores to hold schools, teachers, and students accountable for performance have been adopted in one form or another by all states over the past decade or more. The reauthorization of the Elementary and Secondary Education Act, the No Child Left Behind Act of 2001 (NCLB), made such test-based accountability the crux of national education policy as well. Furthermore, schools and school districts are increasingly using assessment data as a tool for local decisionmaking.

One method for using test-score data to aid in education reform is value-added assessment (VAA).[1] VAA is a collection of complex statistical techniques that uses multiple years of test-score data on students to try to estimate the causal effects of individual schools or teachers on student learning. A method that could truly separate the effects of teachers and schools from the effects of noneducational factors, such as family background, would provide a powerful diagnostic tool and could potentially serve as the basis for individual-level as well as school-level accountability. Because VAA claims to provide such estimates, it has attracted widespread attention from researchers and policymakers. The Tennessee Value-Added Assessment System, or TVAAS (Sanders and Horn, 1998), is the most widely known application of VAA in the United States, and efforts to extend or replicate this model are currently under way in school districts in Dallas, Texas (see Webster et al., 1998), and in other states, including North Carolina, Ohio, and Pennsylvania. In addition, value-added assessment has been used in various countries of the United Kingdom for nearly 20 years.

The value-added information provided to school districts and schools typically includes estimates of the value added by schools to student growth along with information about individual student growth and growth of subgroups of students, such as low-achieving or low-income students. Tennessee and Dallas provide value-added reports for individual teachers, but the other locations mentioned above do not.

As noted in Scheerens, Glas, and Thomas (2003), value-added assessments can support accountability, which involves external monitoring of school performance, or school improvement, which involves internal self-evaluation by school personnel using the data to make better decisions on student placement, curriculum, and practices. The national value-added project in the United Kingdom reports tables of value-added results for all schools, and Tennessee also publicly reports school value-added results. However, in both the United States and the United

---

[1] Value-added assessment is sometimes referred to as value-added analysis, value-added modeling, or growth modeling. Because the Pennsylvania pilot program studied in this report is called the Pennsylvania Value-Added Assessment System, for consistency of terminology within the report, we use the term *value-added assessment* to refer to the value-added information created from test-score data and provided to schools.

Kingdom, most of the focus has been on using the value-added data internally, within local school authorities, to support decisionmaking by educators rather than for external accountability purposes. The utility of VAA for supporting decisionmaking is particularly relevant in today's policy environment. District and school personnel are focusing extensive efforts on raising student achievement on state tests, and recent studies of schools' responses to NCLB suggest that one of the most popular school improvement strategies is the use of achievement data for instructional decisionmaking (Center on Education Policy, 2006; Hamilton et al., 2007).

In theory, VAA can contribute to data-driven decisionmaking in schools, but the specific mechanisms through which VAA would lead to improved student outcomes have not been fully elucidated or explored. In addition, the data on the relationship between implementation of a VAA program and student achievement is limited to a single study, which might not replicate to other settings. The study reported here is designed to address these gaps in our understanding of the relationship between district participation in a VAA system and student achievement. It explores three related questions:

1. What is the effect on student achievement of providing districts with information from a VAA system?
2. How does the use of data by educators whose districts participate in a VAA system differ from that of educators from nonparticipating districts?
3. How do educators respond to the VAA information they receive?

The first question is the causal question of primary interest. The second and third questions are intended to clarify the mechanisms through which provision of VAA information might affect practice and, ultimately, student achievement.

Examining VAA Implementation and Effects

Although few systematic studies have been conducted to examine the effectiveness of data-driven decisionmaking on a large scale, there is some evidence that the use of data can lead to an improved school culture and can contribute to student learning (Feldman and Tung, 2001). In addition, VAA fits into the broader category of test-driven reforms, and there is a mounting body of evidence that the provision of information from standardized tests can lead to significant changes in teachers' instructional practices and content coverage (Hamilton, 2003; Stecher, 2002; Supovitz and Klein, 2003; Symonds, 2003). Whether these practices are desirable or undesirable depends on a number of factors, including educators' capacity to interpret and use data (Choppin, 2002; Marsh, Pane, and Hamilton, 2006; Saunders, 2000). In addition, the end-of-year tests used in most VAA systems may be of less utility for instructional purposes than interim tests that are administered frequently and provide immediate feedback to teachers (Supovitz and Klein, 2003; Symonds, 2003). Therefore, it is important to understand how teachers and principals use VAA information in the context of other data sources.

Very little of the work on educators' use of achievement data has focused specifically on VAA data. Researchers in the United Kingdom have conducted qualitative research on the use of value-added assessments by educators (Saunders, 2000; Scheerens, Glas, and Thomas, 2003, Chapter 17). Scheerens and colleagues describe in detail the use of value-added assessments by the Lancashire Local Education Administration, with a focus on the use of VAA in one school in that district. Administrators report using the VAA data to establish student policies, to assign students to courses, and to set individualized targets for students depending on prior achievement. The case study of one school found that educators used the value-added data extensively and creatively, including discussing the data with individual students. However, this school was selected for the case study because of its active use of the VAA data. In addition, the authors note that the staff at the school were very positive about using data for self-evaluation and improvement, in part because the school recruited teachers who supported this perspective. While the study provides a demonstration of how VAA data might be used in a school where a strong culture of data use exists, it provides little evidence about how providing such data to a cross section of schools will change behavior.

Saunders (2000) reviews qualitative studies on the use of VAA data by educators in various projects in the UK. One study found "peripheral level of awareness" of VAA early in the program but greater awareness after more years of participation (Saunders, 2000, p. 243). However, even among schools that had been participating for several years there was considerable variability in use, and the impact on many department heads had been minimal. There were, however, a few examples of schools making extensive use of the data, similar to those identified by Scheerens, Glas, and Thomas (2003).

Saunders also found in her own case studies lower use of VAA than expected, considerable variability among schools in the use of VAA, and even variability among teachers within schools. At the school level, key factors to using VAA were support by senior management, a championing of VAA data by a senior member of the staff, the school's relative standing on traditional status measures and VAA measures (i.e., schools with poor relative level performance but better relative VAA performance were more likely to use the VAA data), being in the program for at least three years, and receiving some guidance for interpreting the VAA results (Saunders, 2000, p. 247). Saunders concluded that use within the school was driven by staff attitudes and departmental culture.

There has been less research on the use of VAA in the United States. One exception is an evaluation of the effects of VAA on student outcomes in Ohio (Lewis and Ruhil, 2006). Using data from 63 Ohio school districts participating in the School's Online Achievement Results (SOAR) projects and several samples of matched comparison districts, Lewis and Ruhil estimated the effect of receiving the VAA reports on student achievement outcomes. The study explored several matching strategies and used a variety of analytic methods, but all led to the same conclusion: There was no evidence that receiving the VAA report affected fourth or sixth grade student achievement in reading, mathematics, science, or citizenship. Lewis and Ruhil do not provide detailed information on how the VAA data were used by district personnel, principals, or teachers, but they do report that 14 of the 63 SOAR districts were fully implementing VAA through "use at the building level throughout the district by principals and/or teachers to inform decisions about instruction" (Lewis and Ruhil, 2006, p. 5). Lewis and Ruhil compared these districts to matched comparison districts and found that scores for sixth grade students in these districts tend to be statistically significantly higher than students in matched comparison districts. There were no significant differences for fourth graders, and the differences among sixth graders from the two groups were small in all subjects except citizenship when students' prior achievement was included in the model. Thus, the study provides little evidence of the provision of VAA data improving student achievement even among districts that were "fully implementing."

Lewis and Ruhil provide no information on how receiving the VAA reports changed the behaviors or attitudes of educators, including central office administrators, principals, and teachers. The SOAR program was in place only a few years at the time the authors collected their data. Many educators will be unfamiliar with the type of data and reports provided by a VAA system, and with the kinds of practices associated with effective use of data from such a system. Hence, it might take time for the VAA program to affect student outcomes. Prior to that time, however, one might expect changes in educators' attitudes about using data and their practices as a result of using data. An important, missing component from the previous literature is an analysis of the effects of VAA on educators' attitudes and practices.

Another motivation for studying VAA systems is to investigate the value of the information from the value-added measures themselves. Part of the appeal of VAA is the expectation that the method can separate the effects of schools or teachers from the background characteristics of students and thereby provide a better measure of effectiveness of education. Whether value-added measures truly provide measures of the causal effects schools and teachers have on their students has been considerably debated (Braun, 2005; Kupermintz, 2003; McCaffrey et al., 2004a; Raudenbush, 2004; Reckase, 2004). Direct demonstration that value-added measures are truly causal would be very challenging (Rubin, Stuart, and Zanutto, 2004). However, demonstrating that VAA *systems* have causal effects is more straightforward, because the systems may be considered an intervention that can be provided to some schools or districts and not others (Rubin, Stuart, and Zanutto, 2004). If VAA systems have positive effects on student outcomes, then clearly the provision of value-added measures has promise as an intervention. While this would not conclusively show that value-added measures provide estimates of causal effects of schools or teachers, it would suggest that any errors in the measures are sufficiently inconsequential in the context of the VAA system, such that adoption of such systems should be encouraged.

The rollout of the Pennsylvania Value-Added Assessment System (PVAAS) in four waves by the state provided an opportunity to study the effects of VAA systems as an educational intervention. The phased process created a quasi-experimental condition whereby a subset of the school districts participating in PVAAS could be compared to a subset of districts not in the program. This report describes a study of this intervention to address the questions listed above and to attempt to understand the utility of value-added measures of schools. It is important to recognize that this study evaluates a single value-added system during the initial years of pilot implementation. The results might not generalize to other systems and might underestimate the effects of systems in place for longer periods of time. Nevertheless, it provides valuable insights into the effects of value-added systems on educational practice and student outcomes.

Background on Pennsylvania's VAA System

Pennsylvania's adoption of a pilot VAA program provides one opportunity to examine administrators' and teachers' responses to the provision of VAA information. The Pennsylvania Value-Added Assessment System analyzes extant test-score data to produce summary statistics on the performance of schools and students. The information is intended to support decisionmaking about educational programs and practices at the level of the entire district, school, or individual student. SAS, the computer software and analysis corporation hired by the state to conduct the value-added analysis, prepares the summary statistics and presents them to districts through a series of reports available on the Internet. Districts are free to use PVAAS information as they deem appropriate, including deciding whether to make the data accessible to personnel at the school level. PVAAS reports are not used for accountability by the state, and the reports are not available to the public.

This study focuses on the early years of the program, when PVAAS was available to 50 of the state's 501 school districts. These districts comprised the first two cohorts of districts participating in the PVAAS pilot program that ended in fall of 2006, when PVAAS became available to all districts in the state. Because only a subset of the state's school districts participated in the pilot program, others could serve as comparison districts to assess the effects of the VAA on student outcomes and educational practices.

History of PVAAS

With prompting from the Pennsylvania League of Urban Schools, the Pennsylvania Department of Education (PDE) sponsored a program to provide value-added reports to school districts in the state. The program, now referred to as the Pennsylvania Value-Added Assessment System, started with a pilot project that included 32 districts in the spring of 2002.[2] The value-added reports were to be provided by SAS to participating districts each school year. In September 2002, the State Board of Education approved plans to fund PVAAS and developed a plan for rolling it out to remaining districts in the state according to the time line shown in Figure 1.1.

The pilot program began when the state invited Cohort 1 districts to participate in the study. Participation was voluntary, but participating districts were required to conduct districtwide testing at some grades other than 5 and 8 using standardized tests. In the following year additional districts were invited to participate as the second pilot cohort. Again, participation was voluntary and contingent on the Cohort 2 districts conducting district-wide testing using standardized tests.

In summer of 2002, the original 32 pilot districts (Cohort 1 districts) provided SAS with the student test-score data required for creating the PVAAS reports. Because the statewide test, the Pennsylvania System of School Assessment (PSSA), was only administered in a few grades, districts provided scores from other standardized testing programs they had in place at the time. These tests needed to meet three criteria as per SAS quality standards for inclusion in the PVAAS analysis: They had to be aligned to the Pennsylvania Academic Standards, they had to be valid and reliable measures, and they needed to have enough "stretch" to cover the growth of low- and high-achieving students. Some assessments did not meet these criteria. In February 2003, the Cohort 1 districts received hardcopy value-added reports based on their 2001–2002 test-score data. In April 2004, the Cohort 1 districts received their second round of PVAAS reports, based on their 2002–2003 test-score data. These reports were available on the Internet from SAS, but at the time they lacked features that are currently available in the online reports.

---

[2] One of the original districts failed to provide the data necessary to participate in the pilot program and is not included among the 31 Cohort 1 districts used in the current study.

Figure 1.1
Time Line of the PVAAS Rollout

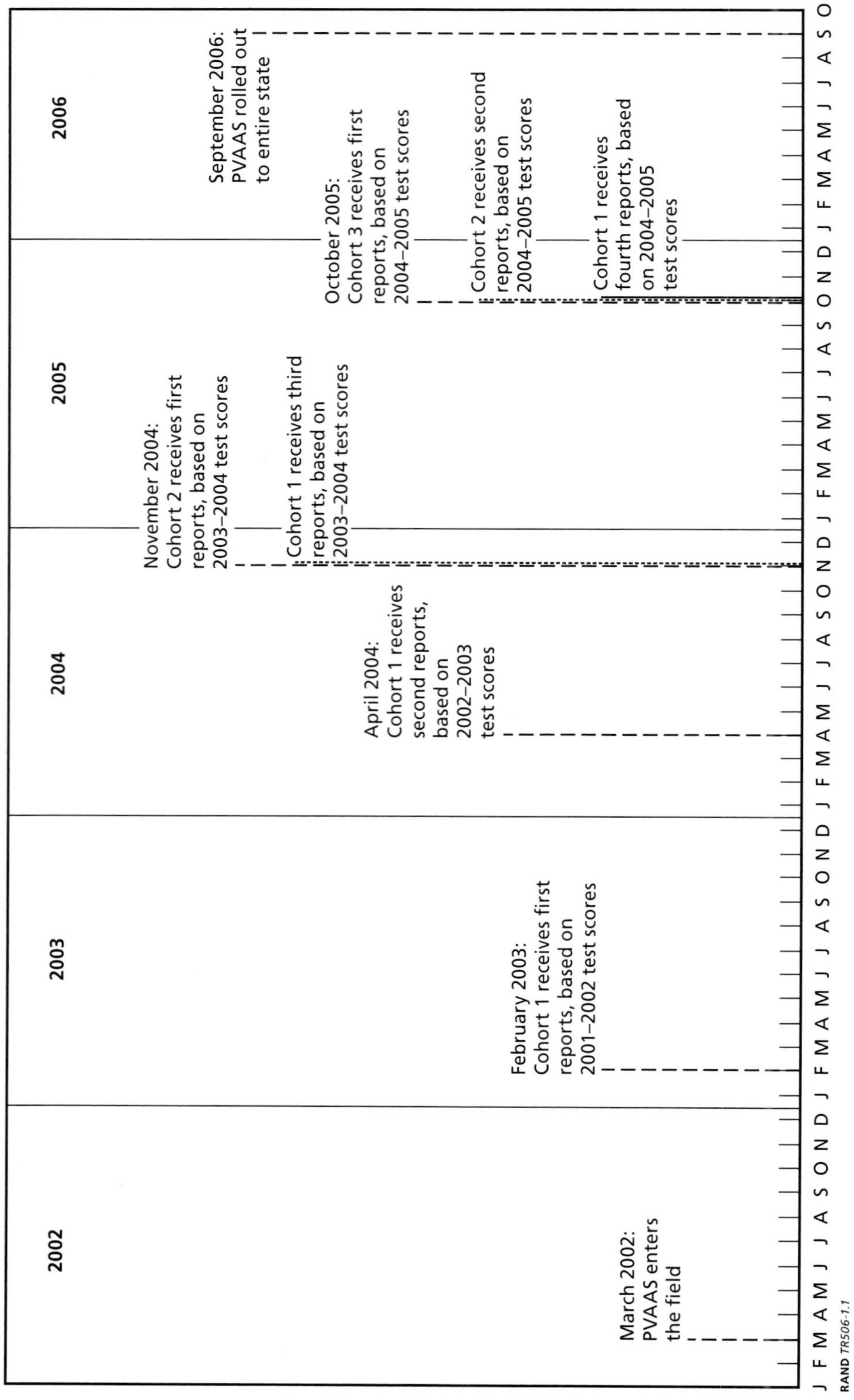

The release of the PVAAS reports in the early years of the pilot occurred late in the school year because of the time necessary for districts to submit the necessary electronic files of historical assessment data to SAS. The data files needed to meet specified formats, with the required fields for longitudinal merging of student assessment records. This proved to be a challenging task for many districts due to a lack of capacity and staff resources to manage these data requirements. In later years, districts completed data preparation in less time and the reports were released earlier in the school year. This data submission protocol used during the pilot program is no longer required for the annual PVAAS reporting.

In November of 2004, Cohort 1 schools received their third reports, based on the 2003–2004 test-score data. At the same time, 19 additional districts from Cohort 2 received PVAAS reports for the first time.[3] The November 2004 reports were fully implemented and contained all or nearly all the features of the PVAAS reporting system described below. In 2005, the program was expanded to include 50 additional Cohort 3 districts, but otherwise the process was the same as in 2004. In 2006, all 501 school districts in the state participated in PVAAS, and for the first time the state's accountability test provided the current year scores for all students in grades 4 and grade 6. Full implementation of PVAAS for grades 4 through 8 will be released in the fall of 2007.

PVAAS Reports

PVAAS provides school districts with a detailed summary of the progress of its students and schools for available grades between 4 and 8.[4] One designated person, for example, the superintendent, in each district receives a secure user name and password for accessing the reports. This account is used to assign all other accounts for users in the district, as determined by the superintendent. Other users might include principals, content leaders, and teachers; who is included is a local district decision.

The school districts in the pilot program received reporting using a different statistical methodology than is currently used in the statewide implementation with all 501 districts. For the purposes of this research report, the reports and statistical methodology used during the pilot phases will be described.

As described in the *Resource Guide for the Pennsylvania Value-Added Assessment System: 2004 PVAAS Reports* (SAS, 2005), the PVAAS reports contain five broad categories of information. The first is what PVAAS calls the Value-Added Report or Value-Added Summary Report (Figure 1.2).[5] These reports provide the value-added effect by grade level and subject (mathematics or reading) of each individual school in the district. Using statistical methods summarized below, SAS uses longitudinal test-score data to estimate each school's contribution

---

3 Cohort 2 included Pittsburgh, Philadelphia, and the Pennsylvania School of the Deaf, along with 16 other districts. Because of the unique characteristics of these districts, they are not included in our study. Unless otherwise stated, references to the Cohort 2 districts exclude these three districts.

4 The grades for which reports were available depended on the districts testing program and these values are not publicly available.

5 We have included reproductions of parts of the PVAAS reports from the time of the pilot study to give readers a clearer understanding of the data received by the districts. These figures do not provide full details on the PVAAS reports or a full view of all features of the report. Readers seeking additional details on the reports should contact the Pennsylvania Department of Education.

Figure 1.2
Example of PVAAS School Value-Added Report from 2003

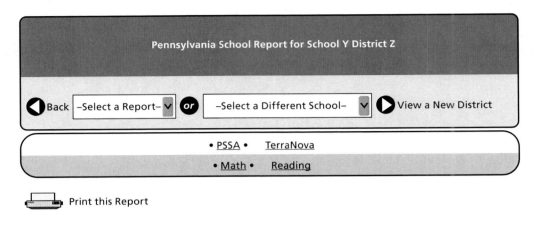

Test	Grade	Year	N	Mean Student Score	Mean Score %tile	Mean Pred Score	Pred. Score %tile	School Effect	Effect Std Err	School vs Testing Pool Avg	Testing Pool
Math	5	2001	20	1513.0	87	1433.8	73	71.9	25.55	Above	TerraNova
		2002	21	1540.1	86	1474.4	76	**54.6**	24.06	Above	TerraNova

RAND *TR506-1.2*

to student achievement gains as distinct from students' background characteristics or previous educational inputs. Each school's effect for a specific subject and grade level is scaled so that 0 indicates that students made standard growth (i.e., grew at a rate that is roughly equivalent to the average student in that grade and subject among districts using the same set of tests). A positive value indicates that the effect for a school in a particular grade level and subject was positive; in other words, students made greater than standard growth. A negative value indicates that students in a particular grade level and subject made less than standard growth. The report also indicates whether each estimated effect is statistically significantly different from zero by providing a designation of above, below, or not detectably different (NDD) from the "testing pool" average. For the pilot districts, standard performance is relative to the schools that administered the same standardized tests (referred to by PVAAS as a "testing pool"). As noted above, because prior to 2006 the state did not have a single accountability test in all grades, PVAAS grouped together schools using the same commercially available standardized tests to fit its models and make its value-added assessments. The reports showed both current year estimates and the historical estimates, so in Figure 1.2 there are two years of estimates because it was the second year of PVAAS reporting.

The second category of information in the PVAAS report is the Diagnostic Report (Figure 1.3), which provides information by subgroups of students defined by achievement level. During the pilot program, achievement level was defined by the quintile of the testing pool distribution of a student's average achievement across all years for which the student has test scores. Values are reported separately by grade and subject. The reported values are the

Figure 1.3
Example of PVAAS Diagnostic Report from 2003

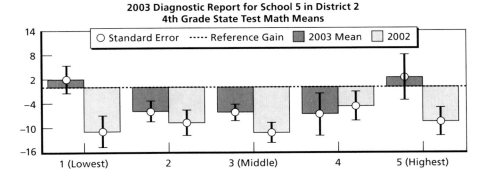

2003 Diagnostic Report for School 5 in District 2
4th Grade State Test Math Means

			Observed minus Predicted Score by Predicted Score Quintile				
			1 (Lowest)	2	3 (Middle)	4	5 (Highest)
Math	2003	Mean	2.0	−5.9	−6.3	−6.7	2.4
		Std Err	3.4	2.6	2.1	5.2	5.6
		Nr of Students	18	21	19	12	6
		% of Students	23.7	27.6	25.0	15.8	7.9
	2002	Mean	−10.8	−8.7	−11.2	−4.7	−8.5
		Std Err	3.9	3.1	2.4	3.6	3.4
		Nr of Students	18	20	23	15	8
		% of Students	21.4	23.8	27.4	17.9	9.5

⊞ View Performance Diagnostics Report

Need help interpreting this report? <u>Hints</u>
RAND *TR506-1.3*

average gain scores for students in the group. Values are presented in tabular and graphical formats.

The third category of information in the PVAAS report is the Performance Diagnostic Report (Figure 1.4). These reports are similar to the Diagnostic Reports except that the groups are defined by predicted proficiency level for the current year score on the state's accountability test rather than quintiles of average achievement.

The fourth category of information in the PVAAS report is the Student Report (Figure 1.5). These reports include individual students' observed test scores and their expected or predicted test scores, which are based on test scores from other grades and the district average for all students as a point of reference. The predicted values are not shown in Figure 1.5 because this feature was added to the reports after 2003.

The final category of information in the PVAAS report is the Student Projection Report (Figure 1.6). The report presents students' predicted performance on future state tests (i.e., the Pennsylvania System of School Assessment) at higher grade levels. For example, for a student in seventh grade, the Student Projection Report would provide his or her predicted score on the eighth-grade PSSA. The report provides both the predicted percentile on the test and the predicted probability that the student's score will fall into a user-specified performance category, for example, that the student exceeds the proficient level.

All the reports are interactive and allow users to probe for additional information about students and schools. The reporting system also includes a hints page to assist users. The reports provide no summary statistics for individual teachers. Moreover, the reports provide no specific instructions for how districts should respond to the information in the reports. Recently PDE

Figure 1.4
Example of PVAAS Performance Diagnostic Report from 2003

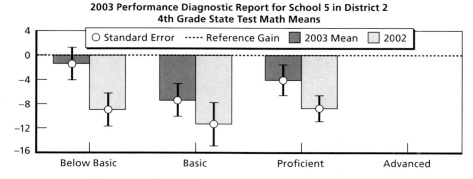

			Observed minus Predicted Score by Predicted Proficiency Group			
			Below Basic	Basic	Proficient	Advanced
Math	2003	Mean	−1.4	−7.4	−4.1	
		Std Err	2.7	2.7	2.5	
		Nr of Students	30	16	29	1
		% of Students	39.5	21.1	38.2	1.3
	2002	Mean	−8.9	−11.3	−8.7	
		Std Err	2.7	3.6	2.1	
		Nr of Students	31	14	35	4
		% of Students	36.9	16.7	41.7	4.8

▦ View School Diagnostics Report

RAND *TR506-1.4*

Figure 1.5
Example of PVAAS Student Report from 2002

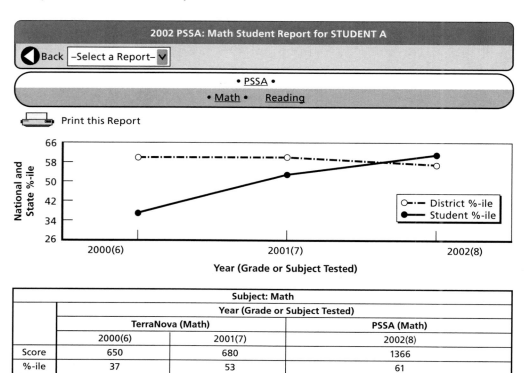

	TerraNova (Math)		PSSA (Math)
	2000(6)	2001(7)	2002(8)
Score	650	680	1366
%-ile	37	53	61

RAND *TR506-1.5*

Figure 1.6
Example of PVAAS Student Projection Report from 2003

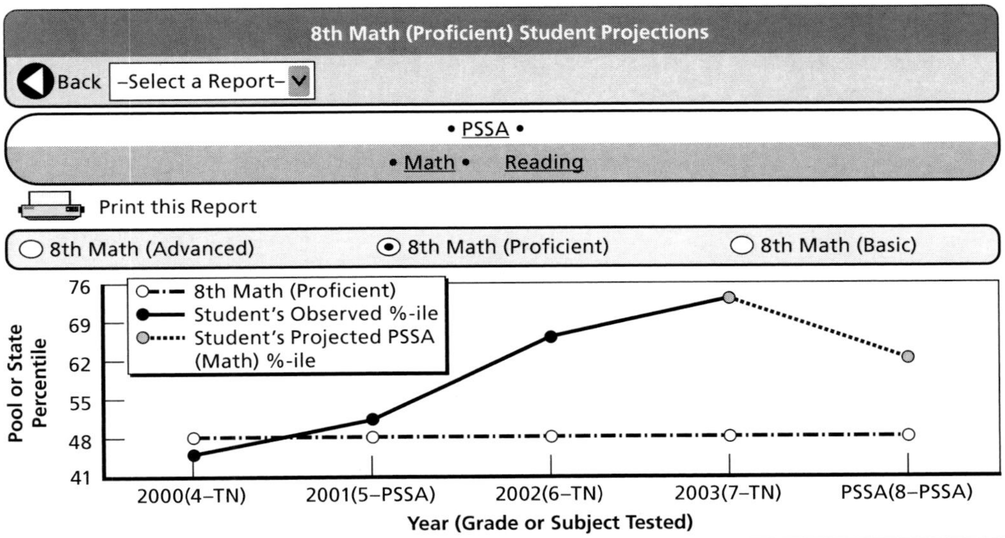

	Subject: 8th Math (Proficient)				
	Year (Grade or Subject Tested)				
	TerraNova (Math)	PSSA (Math)	TerraNova (Math)		8th Math (Proficient)
	2000(4)	2001(5)	2002(6)	2003(7)	Projection (Probability) (Grade – 8)
Score	629	1316	689	706	
%-ile	45	51	66	73	62 (79.8%)

RAND *TR506-1.6*

has added more information about PVAAS on its Web site, including information on using reports for data-driven decisionmaking, but most of this information did not exist during the pilot program.

At the time of data collection for this study, three text resources were available from the state[6]:

1. *Introductory Guide for Pennsylvania Educators Understanding Value-Added Analysis: A Measure of Progress and Growth*, a 16-page introduction to the Pennsylvania value-added models prepared by Battelle for Kids, a nonprofit organization established to promote the use of value-added assessment in Ohio. This brochure provides a layman's introduction to value-added assessment. It describes the differences between students' achievement levels and progress or growth. It contains simple examples to demonstrate the concepts and includes many testimonials on the utility of value-added assessment. It also provides a history and statement that the intent of the PVAAS program is to provide an additional tool to aid local school district decisionmaking, and that PVAAS is not intended for teacher accountability.
2. *Resource Guide for the Pennsylvania Value-Added Assessment System*, a notebook-style publication created by SAS as a training and reference resource. It contains details

[6] As of September 2007, versions of these three documents are available on the Pennsylvania Training and Technical Assistance Network Web site (undated). However, the documents have been updated and clearly differ from the versions that were available to educators at the time of this study.

on accessing the online reporting system and the reports, and includes demonstration screen shots. It also includes testimonials and anecdotes about the benefits of value-added assessment. It does not provide detailed guidance on using the PVAAS reports for educational decisionmaking.

3. "PVAAS Overview," an introductory PowerPoint presentation that presents much of the same information documented in the other two documents.

PVAAS Statistical Methodology for the Pilot Program

The key components of the PVAAS reports are the school value-added reports and the individual student projections. These values are estimated using a complex statistical procedure[7] that uses students' prior test scores to predict their current or future performance. The model used is

$$Y = m + b_1(X_1 - \overline{X_1}) + \ldots + b_k(X_k - \overline{X_k}) + e \qquad (1)$$

where Y is the score of interest (e.g., the current math score or the score on the future PSSA), and X_1 to X_k are prior test scores. The Xs can be for the same subject as Y or for other subjects. PVAAS requires three prior scores for estimation. $\overline{X_1}$ to $\overline{X_k}$ are the means for the prior scores for the average school within the testing pool. The means for the average school, or the average school means, are the averages of the individual school means. Because of missing data due to student transfers and other reasons, not all students have all of the prior-year test scores. PVAAS uses all the available data to estimate the model coefficients using standard methods for incomplete data (Schafer, 2002; Wright, Sanders, and Rivers, 2006).[8] PVAAS accounts for the clustering of students within schools by estimating coefficients using pooled-within-school data, so differences in the current-year (or future-year) scores and prior-year scores across schools are not used in the estimation. Using the resulting coefficient estimates and all the available data for each student, PVAAS predicts students' performance on current (or future) tests.

For the school value-added reports, PVAAS subtracts the predicted score for the current test from the student's observed score on that test to estimate the residual of how much the student achieved above or below expectation. PVAAS then averages these residuals by grade within school to obtain the school's value-added measure for each grade.[9]

Individual student reports present the predicted values and projections to future scores. Predictions and projections depend on the population mean chosen (m in Equation 1). PVAAS uses the average school means when making predictions, and depending on the nature of the

---

[7]   Starting with the 2005–2006 school year, Pennsylvania administered the PSSA in reading and mathematics in grades 3 to 8. PVAAS methodology changed in response to the change in testing. Methods described here refer to the methods used during the pilot period. Details on the current PVAAS methodology should be obtained from the Pennsylvania Department of Education.

[8]   PVAAS estimates the covariance matrix for the outcome and prior year scores by maximizing the incomplete data likelihood using the EM algorithm (Wright, Sanders, and Rivers, 2006).

[9]   We could not find explicit details on the exact methods used by PVAAS, so it is unclear if the raw average is reported or if the average is scaled by a value less than one ("shrunken") to reduce the sampling variance in the estimate. For the Tennessee Value-Added Assessment System, raw averages are used for schools and we expect the same is true for PVAAS.

report will use the average school mean or the means for the school the student is likely to attend when projecting to future scores. For example, when projecting to performance on an eighth grade test for an elementary school student, PVAAS will use the mean for the middle school the student is most likely to attend as suggested by historical school progression patterns.

As discussed earlier, during the pilot program Pennsylvania did not have a statewide test in grades 3 to 8. Hence, PVAAS used tests administered by the local districts to make the predictions and other value-added measures. School districts administering the same commercial standardized tests were pooled together for fitting models. Average school means were based on the schools in the pool of districts administering the same test. If the pool changed as additional schools were added with the rollout of the program to Cohorts 2 and 3, schools' performance could change. In addition, PVAAS rescaled scores prior to fitting models, but the details of the rescaling are not available in documentation and papers describing the PVAAS methods.

Organization of This Report

The remainder of the report is presented in six chapters. The next chapter provides an overview of the data and analytic methods used to evaluate the effect of PVAAS on students and educators. Chapter Three reports findings on the effects of PVAAS on student test scores. Chapters Four, Five, and Six present findings on the effects of PVAAS on district personnel, principals, and teachers, respectively. Each of these three chapters first compares the response of educators from PVAAS districts to their counterparts in matched comparison districts to estimate the effects of the program, then presents summaries of the ways educators in PVAAS districts report using the PVAAS information. The final chapter summarizes our findings and discusses their policy implications.

CHAPTER TWO

Methods and Data

The primary goal of the study is to estimate the causal effects of VAA on student achievement and educational practice using the PVAAS pilot program. Because the pilot districts were not randomly chosen, the study uses a quasi-experimental design. We use matching methods to identify comparison districts that are similar to the pilot districts so that differences in student outcomes and educational practice can be treated as estimates of the causal effects of the pilot program.

The study uses two types of outcomes: standardized achievement test scores to estimate the effects on student achievement, and survey responses from district administrators, principals, and teachers to estimate effects on educational practice.

This chapter describes our methods for matching districts, our methods for modeling test scores, and our approach to sampling and analyzing the survey responses. It also describes the test-score data and the survey instruments.

Details on Matching

Overview of Matching Approach

In quasi-experimental studies such as the evaluation of the PVAAS pilot program, units (e.g., school districts) are not randomly assigned to experimental conditions, and thus the units in the various experimental groups can differ on covariates (i.e., pretreatment factors) that may be related to outcomes. Adjustment for these pretreatment differences must be made—otherwise they may confound the estimated program effects, which in turn could lead to making incorrect inferences about the effects of PVAAS.

The current study matched the pilot districts to other Pennsylvania school districts that were not involved in the pilot study but were similar to the pilot districts in terms of a large number of preexisting matching variables. The study team chose variables for matching with input from a diverse group, including stakeholders, and it selected the matched comparison sample prior to obtaining any outcomes data. This ensured that the choice of the sample was not in any way influenced by the potential results of the study (Rubin, 2001).

Matching Variables

We collected an extensive dataset of covariates on all Pennsylvania school districts. The variables, selected on an a priori basis by the project team in consultation with the members of the Pennsylvania State Education Association (PSEA), were chosen because they were believed to be likely predictors of student achievement and descriptors of the overall nature of the districts. The variables included

- district financial and staffing variables, such as instructional expenses, the taxable property value of the district, district size (average daily attendance), teacher salaries, number of teachers, teacher tenure (average years of service), local tax revenues and efforts (taxes per market value of the taxable properties), and pupil-teacher ratio
- proportion of students whose families receive support through the federally funded Temporary Assistance for Needy Families (TANF) program
- racial distributions obtained from the Common Core of Data for 2001
- the low-income distributions from the Pennsylvania Department of Education Web site for the 10 years prior to PVAAS
- 2000 Census variables on the employment, education, and income of the population living within each school district, as well as property values, rents, and the proportion of female-headed households in the area
- Mathematics and Reading PSSA achievement test scale scores for fifth-, eighth-, and eleventh-grade students for 1998 to 2003, obtained from the state's Web site. We also estimated linear growth in scores for every district by subject and grade.

Three potentially important types of information were unavailable for use in the matching: information about the district testing programs, information about the tenure of the superintendent, and information about individual student growth. Testing was a requirement of PVAAS and would have been a useful control. District leadership is important for program implementation, and data on tenure would also have been useful. Because PVAAS emphasizes growth, matching on student growth might have been valuable.

All variables used in the matching were measured before the districts began participating in PVAAS. For Cohort 1 districts, which began participating in the 2002–2003 school year, variables were measured through the 2001–2002 school year. For Cohort 2, which began in the 2003–2004 school year, all variables used in matching were measured before the fall of 2003. Even though the first reports for this cohort were delayed until fall of 2004, these districts were scheduled to receive reports in the 2003–2004 school year and were actively working with SAS and the state during that year. Moreover, we were unaware of the delays in reporting until after data collection began.

We conducted extensive exploratory data analyses to select transformations of variables, identify outliers, and choose the exact subsets of these highly correlated variables for use in the matching procedure. For example, the low-income data had correlations of about .99 across years, and we chose to include in the analyses only data from the most recent year. In the end, there were approximately 100 variables for which it would be desirable to obtain good matches, and we identified approximately 20 of those as being particularly important. We highlighted the district average test scores as being particularly important because of their correlation with other educational measures, and because test scores would be an important outcome in the estimation of the impacts of the PVAAS pilot. Other variables chosen as important included the trends or slopes in scores, the percentage of white students in the district, average educational expenses, the pupil-teacher ratio, and education levels of the population from the census.

Matching Methods for Cohort 1

The matching procedure selected sets of comparison districts for the districts in Cohorts 1 and 2 of the PVAAS pilot, with the matching for each cohort done completely separately. We first describe the method for selecting the matches for Cohort 1, and then describe the method for Cohort 2. The cohorts required different methods due to the very small number of districts in Cohort 2.

For Cohort 1 we decided to select one matched comparison district for each pilot district. Alternative matching schemes, such as matching multiple comparison units to the same pilot district, matching multiple pilot districts to the same comparison district, or weighting the entire comparison sample, might also have been used. Allowing for other than one-to-one matching can sometimes provide samples that are more similar than one-to-one matching (Dehejia and Wahba, 2002). We explored matching that allowed multiple comparisons units to a single comparison district, but it did not lead to significant improvement. Moreover, matching multiple pilot districts to the same comparison district would have reduced our sample of comparison districts and inflated the variance of our estimates. This loss in sample and consequent loss in power for testing for PVAAS effects might have offset any reductions in bias that the more flexible matching might have allowed. Matching multiple comparisons districts to each pilot district could have yielded a larger sample of comparison districts and improved the power of tests. However, the gains in power would have been small, and increasing districts would have increased data collection costs. Hence we chose one-to-one matching.

To select the 31 non-PVAAS districts most similar to the 31 PVAAS districts in Cohort 1, we used a two-part procedure for matching. The first step restricted the potential matches to those with propensity scores similar to the pilot districts, as a way of selecting districts with similar covariate values. The second step prioritized close matches on particularly important covariates such as prior year test scores. In the end, the matching procedure selected the 31 comparison districts that minimized the average covariate distance between the pilot districts and the selected matches, leading to matched samples with very similar covariate distributions. We now describe these two steps in more detail.

We first estimated a propensity score model using the 31 Cohort 1 districts and the other districts eligible to be used as matches (we excluded as possible matches the districts in PVAAS Cohorts 2 and 3). The propensity score estimation procedure used logistic regression to estimate the probability of being in Cohort 1 given the chosen set of covariates. The logistic regression model assumes that the probability that a school district with a given vector of background characteristics, X, is in the pilot program is given by the following equation:

$$\text{Probability of being in the pilot given } X = \frac{e^{x'\beta}}{1 + e^{x'\beta}} \qquad (2)$$

where β is a vector of parameters that are estimated from the data to provide propensity scores. Given this equation the natural logarithm of the odds of the propensity score (the ratio of the probability of being in the pilot to the probability of not being in the pilot) equals $X'\beta$.

A model selection process determined the best variables (including quadratic terms and two-way interactions) for inclusion in the model (see, e.g., Dehejia and Wahba, 1999); because of the small number of pilot districts, only a small number of variables could be included. The final model used 14 variables—12 2002 test-score variables (six means from 2002 and six associated slopes for linear growth in scores from spring of 1998 to spring of 2002) as well as the percentage of white students in the district in 2001 and a measure of per-pupil expenditures.[1]

The matching itself was done using Mahalanobis matching within propensity score "calipers" (Rubin and Thomas, 2000), where the Mahalanobis distance was calculated using the 14 variables mentioned above.[2] The propensity score (Rosenbaum and Rubin, 1983) equals the probability that a district with given values of the matching variables participates in the pilot program. The caliper required that districts be matched to one another only if the log-odds of their propensity scores were within 0.25 standard deviations units.[3] Within these calipers, the best match for each Cohort 1 district was chosen to minimize the sum of the Mahalanobis distances between each Cohort 1 district and its matched partner. Procedures such as this, which optimize a global distance measure, generally yield better matches than do the standard greedy matching algorithms that match each treated unit one at a time and do not consider a global distance measure (Gu and Rosenbaum, 1993; Rosenbaum, 2002). In this way, we chose the 31 control districts that were the most similar to the PVAAS Cohort 1 districts in terms of minimizing the sum of the Mahalanobis distances.

One aspect of this optimal matching algorithm is that, because it attempts to find the best overall sample rather than finding the best match for each Cohort 1 district, not every individual matched pair would seem like an ideal pairing to people familiar with the districts. However, the matched sample we obtained yields smaller standardized bias (more similar covariate distributions) than would a sample chosen to match each pilot district to its closest nonpilot district.[4] In addition, our chosen sample contains 31 comparison districts. If we gave each pilot district its closest match, we would select only 26 districts, because several pilots share a closest match. As demonstrated below, the set of matched comparison districts and the set of pilot districts look very similar and are more balanced than they would likely have been had the 62 matched districts (31 Cohort 1 and 31 matched comparison districts) been randomly assigned to the pilot or comparison conditions.

We also explored alternative matching procedures, including propensity score matching with no Mahalanobis matching, Mahalanobis matching using only the pretreatment variables themselves, and Mahalanobis matching using both the pretreatment variables and the propen-

---

[1]   The measure of per-pupil expenditures was the actual instructional expense per weighted average daily membership. Weighted average daily membership is the pupil count for a district, weighted by grade level. In Pennsylvania, for each 180 days attendance, secondary students (grades 7–12) are counted as 1.36; elementary pupils (grades 1–6) are counted as 1.00; and one-half-time kindergarten students are counted as .50.

[2]   The Mahalanobis distance is a multivariate distance measure that scales the squared difference in means of the covariates by the variance-covariance matrix of those covariates. Specifically, the Mahalanobis distance between groups 1 and 2 is calculated as $(\mu_1 - \mu_2)\Sigma^{-1}(\mu_1 - \mu_2)$, where μ_i is the vector of means of the covariates in group i and Σ is the variance-covariance matrix of the covariates, calculated in group 1 (the PVAAS districts, in this case). This distance measure equals the weighted sum of squares of the differences in covariate vectors, where the covariate vectors have been transformed such that the elements have variance equal to one and zero correlation.

[3]   If ρ denotes the propensity score for a district, then the log-odds of the propensity score equal $\ln(\rho /\{1 - \rho\})$, where $\ln()$ is the natural logarithm function. The propensity score and log-odds were calculated for all districts in the state, and the standard deviation of these values were used in the calipers.

[4]   The standardized bias for a particular covariate is defined as the difference in means between the treated group (e.g., Cohort 1 districts) and the control group (e.g., the matched comparison districts), divided by the standard deviation of that covariate in the treated group.

sity score. However, the procedure based on Mahalanobis matching on the test-score variables within propensity score calipers provided the best balance on all the covariates.

Matching Methods for Cohort 2

Because there were only 16 districts in Cohort 2, and because the covariate distributions of the Cohort 2 pilot districts were very similar to those for the full set of potential comparison districts, the matching algorithm used for the Cohort 1 districts was unable to find a set of 16 comparison districts that adequately matched the pilot districts. The means of the covariates in the matched samples chosen by the algorithm used for Cohort 1 were farther from the means for the pilot districts than were the covariate means for the full set of potential comparison districts. This type of small-sample lack of balance also occurs in randomized experiments with few units randomized to treatment and control conditions, where there are sometimes large differences in the covariates due solely to chance. Given that the algorithm described above failed to find an acceptable set of matched districts, selecting matches for the Cohort 2 districts required an alternative approach.

To find a set of comparison districts that were similar to the 16 Cohort 2 districts, we drew 100,000 random samples of 16 districts from the set of potential matches and chose the random sample that yielded the best "balance" between the Cohort 2 districts and the matched comparison districts. Specifically, we first selected from the 100,000 samples approximately 280 samples that had the smallest distance between the sampled districts and the districts in Cohort 2. This multivariate distance was defined as the sum of squares of the differences in covariate vectors, where the vectors have been transformed such that the elements have variance one and zero correlation. For each of these 280 samples, we then computed the average across all covariates of the absolute standardized difference in means between the sample and the Cohort 2 districts. We identified three with the best balance in terms of these standardized mean differences. For these three samples, we investigated the standardized mean differences for individual key covariates (e.g., prior test scores) and calculated other measures of balance to choose the one matched sample that provided the best match to the pilot districts.

Unlike the matches for Cohort 1, the matches chosen for Cohort 2 do not form individual matched pairs with particular pilot districts. Rather, we selected a sample in which the group of 16 districts was similar overall to the group of 16 Cohort 2 districts. Because our interest is in estimating the overall effect of the PVAAS pilot program, the lack of individual matched pairs does not prohibit estimation of the effects of interest. If a chosen matched district did not respond to our request for data, we selected as a replacement the district not yet contacted that made the revised comparison sample the most similar to the pilot sample. We note again that all of this matching was done without any access to the outcome variables, and thus there was no potential for choosing a particular set of matches to produce a desired result. This is equivalent to the practice of balancing means in randomized experiments (Greenberg, 1953).

Matching Results for Cohort 1

We were able to find a set of 31 comparison districts that were very similar to the 31 Cohort 1 PVAAS districts. The list of Cohort 1 districts and their matches is given in Table A.1 of

Appendix A. As described above, we used the standardized bias as a measure of the "balance" (similarity) of the covariates in the groups. The standardized bias is calculated for each covariate as the difference in means in the two groups, divided by the standard deviation in the set of PVAAS Cohort 1 districts. Dividing by the standard deviation puts the differences in means onto the same scale for each covariate (number of standard deviations), and using the standard deviation in the Cohort 1 districts means that the standardized bias is not directly affected by changes in sample sizes between the full and matched samples. As a generally accepted rule of thumb, well-matched samples should have an average absolute standardized bias of substantially less than 0.25 (one-quarter of a standard deviation). Standardized biases greater than 0.5 are particularly large and indicate large differences between the groups.

The box plots in Figure 2.1 show the standardized biases of the approximately 100 covariates in the full samples (the 31 Cohort 1 districts compared with the 404 non-PVAAS districts eligible to be chosen as a match), as well as the standardized biases in the matched samples. In each group, the upper end of the box is the 75th percentile of the distribution of standardized bias values across the covariates. The line in the center of the box is the median, and the low end of the box is the 25th percentile of the standardized biases. Ideally the box would be very tight around zero, indicating that across the covariates the differences between the groups would be consistently small. The lines above and below the boxes indicate about the 5th and 95th percentiles in the distribution of standardized biases, and the circles indicate outliers that are far from rest of the distribution. We see that the standardized biases are more tightly clustered around 0 in the matched samples, with no standardized bias greater than 0.5, as compared with quite a few standardized biases over 0.25 in the full sample. Figure A.1 in Appendix A presents histograms of the standardized biases.

Tables A.2 and A.3 also present the reduction in bias achieved by the matching method for the full set of covariates. On most variables, substantial bias reduction resulted, with 79 percent of covariates having smaller absolute standardized bias in the matched samples as compared with the full samples. Overall, before matching, the average absolute standardized bias in the 100 covariates and the propensity score was 0.24, with a range of 0.01 to 1.15 (median=0.22). After matching, the average absolute bias in these 101 variables was 0.10, with a range of 0.00 to 0.36 (median=0.07).

There were five variables with moderate standardized biases (i.e., over .25 in absolute value) in the matched sample:

- Grade 5 Math, Time Trend in PSSA Score, Slope   0.36
- Percentage of Women with 0–8 Years of Education   0.32
- Grade 11 Math, Time Trend in PSSA Score, Slope   0.29
- Grade 5 Reading, Time Trend in PSSA Score, Slope   0.28
- Teacher Average Years of Experience   0.28

The test-score variables are somewhat problematic because grade 5 math, grade 11 math, and grade 5 reading test scores grew slower on average for the matched comparison districts than for the pilot districts. Cohort 1 includes some of the lowest-performing districts in the state, which contributes to the remaining differences between pilot and matched comparison districts. Linear analysis of covariance can be used in the analysis of outcomes to correct for these remaining differences, assuming approximate linearity. We explored the sensitivity of results to models that do and do not control for the three test-score slope variables, average

**Figure 2.1
Cohort 1 Box Plots Showing Balance of Covariates Before and After Matching**

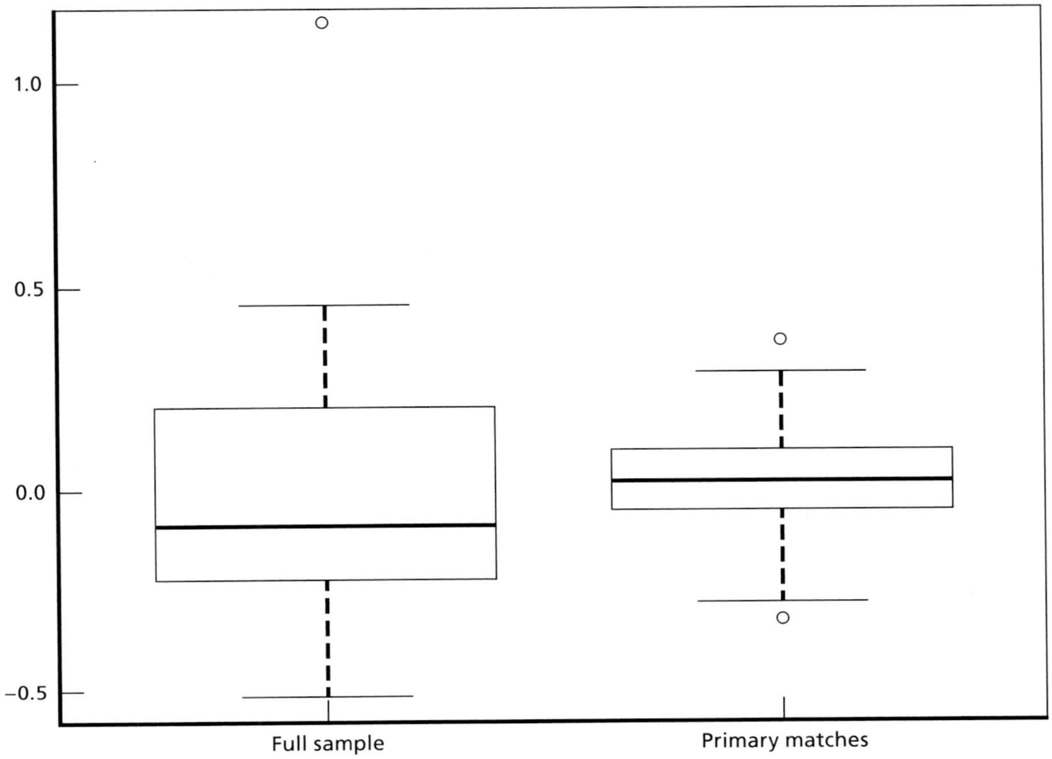

years of teaching experience in the district, and the percentage of women with eight or fewer years of education.

Figure 2.2 illustrates the balance as measured by the standardized bias between pilot and comparison districts for our sample compared with samples that might occur had 31 of these 62 districts been randomly assigned to the pilot condition. We conducted 5,000 random assignments of these districts. The six panels in the figure correspond to different summaries across the 101 variables (100 covariates and propensity scores) of the absolute standardized bias. Each panel contains a histogram showing the distribution of the summary statistics for the 5,000 alternative random assignments. Also in each panel is a vertical line indicating the value of the summary for our matched sample. For all six panels the vertical line is at the extreme left of the histogram. Thus, according to any of these six measures, the balance we obtain with our matched sample is better than we would be likely to obtain through a randomized experiment with these 62 districts.

Matching Results for Cohort 2

The list of PVAAS Cohort 2 pilot and matched comparison districts is given in Table A.4 of Appendix A. As was shown for Cohort 1, the box plots in Figure 2.3 show the standardized biases of the approximately 100 covariates in the full sample (the 16 Cohort 2 districts compared with the 404 non-PVAAS districts eligible to be chosen as a match) as well as the stan-

Figure 2.2
Histograms of Summary Statistics for Absolute Standardized Bias for 5,000 Random Assignments of the 62 Pilot and Matched Comparison Districts

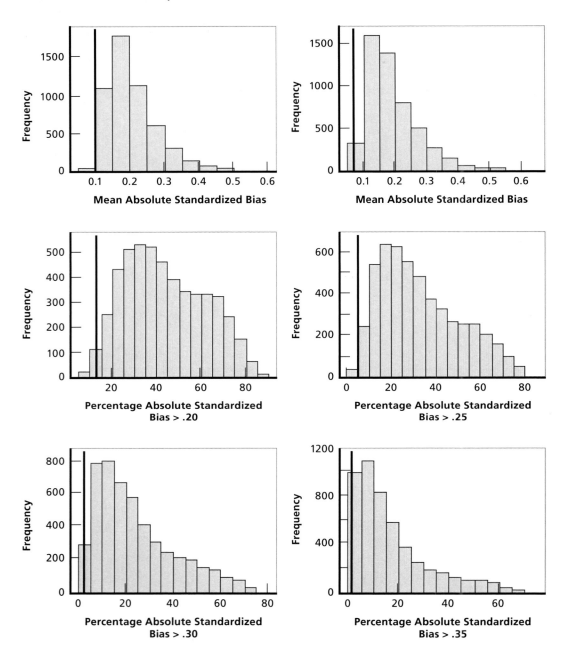

NOTE: The vertical line in each panel is the summary statistic for the actual observed assignments.
RAND TR506-2.2

dardized biases in the matched samples. In contrast with the situation seen for Cohort 1, we see that, even before the matching, the set of Cohort 2 districts looks similar to the full set of non-PVAAS districts, with fairly small standardized biases. The matching selects a set of 16

Figure 2.3
Cohort 2 Box Plots Showing Balance Before and After Matching

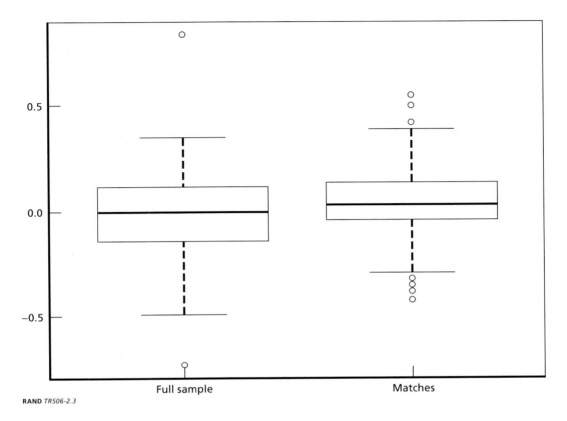

RAND TR506-2.3

districts that also have good balance with the Cohort 2 districts. Figure A.2 in Appendix A presents histograms of the standardized biases.

Tables A.5 and A.6 of Appendix A demonstrate the reduction in bias achieved by the matching method for the full set of covariates. Again, the balance before and after matching is similar, with 52 percent of covariates having smaller absolute standardized bias in the matched samples compared with the full samples. Overall, the average absolute standardized bias in the 106 covariates[5] and the propensity score before matching was 0.15, with a range of 0.01 to 0.84 (median=0.12). After matching, the average absolute standardized bias in the 106 covariates and the propensity score was 0.13, with a range of 0.00 to .55 (median=0.11).

Fifteen variables have moderate or larger (greater than .25 in absolute value) standardized bias in the matched sample:

- Percentage of Women with 13–15 Years of Education   0.55
- Log(Population/Mile²)   0.50
- Time Trend Slope, Grade 5 Reading   0.42
- Transformed Average Teacher Salary   0.39
- Average Teacher Salary   0.31
- Percentage of Men with 13–15 Years of Education   0.30

---

[5]   The 2003 data included reading and mathematics test scores from 2003, increasing the number of covariates to 106.

- Percentage of Black Students   0.28
- Percentage Urban   0.25
- Log(Percentage of White Students)   −0.27
- Percentage of White Students   −0.27
- Percentage Not in Labor Force   −0.29
- Percentage Vacant Houses   −0.32
- Percentage of Women Not in Labor Force   −0.35
- Percentage of Women with 0–8 Years of Education   −0.38
- Percentage of Men with 9–11 Years of Education   −0.42

Only one of the variables is a test-score variable. Most of the others are demographic variables, which have a somewhat less direct relationship to educational achievement than do prior test scores. There is also a moderate difference in average teacher salaries across the two groups. We tested the sensitivity of our results to linear covariate adjustments for these variables.[6]

Figure A.3 replicates Figure 2.2 for the Cohort 2 samples. Again we conducted 5,000 random assignments of the 32 districts in the sample (16 Cohort 2 pilot districts and the 16 matched comparison districts) and find that our matched sample is better balanced than might be expected from a small randomized trial with these 32 districts.

The Pennsylvania System of School Assessment (PSSA)

Of primary interest to our study is the effect of VAA on student outcomes. Although many outcomes are of interest, students' scores on standardized achievement tests currently receive the most attention from policymakers and the public, in part because of weight given to these scores by state accountability systems in response to NCLB. Interest in achievement tests goes beyond their role in accountability and the assessment of schools' current performance. Researchers also use achievement tests as proxies for other, longer-term measures of the effects of the educational system. Test scores are especially useful because they tend to correlate with outcomes such as employment or earnings, but are available much sooner than these other types of data. For these reasons, this study uses the Pennsylvania state achievement test scores—the Pennsylvania System of School Assessment—as its measure of student outcomes. We examine PSSA mathematics and reading scores for students in grades 5 and 8 from 2004 and 2005. These were the only grades within the grade span covered by PVAAS that were tested in mathematics and reading during these school years.

The PSSA is an excellent measure for this study. Because it is the state's accountability test, it is of great importance to educators and policymakers in the state. The PSSA is the only test administered to students from all school districts in Pennsylvania, including both the pilot and comparison districts. In addition, PVAAS measures are based in part on the PSSA test scores, so we would expect that the PSSA could be responsive to actions taken on the basis of PVAAS.

The mathematics test is designed to measure students' ability to understand mathematical processes, solve problems, and recall information. The reading test measures students' reading

---

[6]   As described below, because of the small sample size, we could not include all these variables in our analyses, and we conducted exploratory analyses to pick the subset that was correlated with outcomes prior to testing model sensitivity.

comprehension through a series of questions linked to brief reading passages. The questions ask students to recall specific information from the passages and to make inferences on the basis of that information.

All the PSSA tests are matrix sampled, meaning that a set of core items is given given to all students and other sets of items are completed by samples of students. Our analysis uses the individual student scores, which are based only on the core items.

Both the mathematics and reading tests consist of multiple-choice and constructed-response items. The multiple-choice items are scored dichotomously. In mathematics, the open-ended items are scored on a five-point scale (0 to 4) by raters using a standardized scoring rubric. In reading, the open-ended items are scored on a four-point scale (0 to 3) using the Pennsylvania Reading Assessment Rubric. For both subjects, the majority of items are multiple-choice items. For both reading and mathematics, the core items include three or four opened-ended items and from 40 to 60 multiple-choice items depending on the year, grade level, and subject. The reliability of the individual student scores is very high, ranging from .91 to .94 across years, grade levels, and subjects.

Methods for Estimating the Effects of PVAAS on PSSA Scores

We estimated and tested the effect of the PVAAS pilot program on student achievement using a series of models for PSSA test scores. Models were estimated separately for reading and mathematics, for each grade and year of data, and for Cohorts 1 and 2. We used separate models for each grade and year to allow for changes in the tests, and because Lewis and Ruhil (2006) found in Ohio that differences between VAA and comparison students were sensitive to students' years of exposure to VAA. PVAAS was just starting at the time our test-score data were collected; therefore, each successive cohort of students had an additional year of exposure to PVAAS and could potentially show greater effects of the program. Similarly, Cohort 2 had two fewer years of experience with PVAAS than Cohort 1, and results could differ by cohort.

Every model included an indicator for PVAAS status (pilot or comparison district). The first model used data aggregated to the mean for each district by grade (5 or 8). The difference between the mean for the pilot districts and the comparison districts estimated the effect of the PVAAS program. A standard t-test tested the significance of the effect. To check the sensitivity of our findings to the assumptions of the standard t-test, we tested pilot program effects using common nonparametric procedures (Wilcoxan Rank-Sum Test).

Because districts vary in size, the aggregate data can provide inefficient estimates of the effect of PVAAS on individual students. Hierarchical models provide more efficient estimates (Raudenbush and Bryk, 2002). Using individual test scores, we fit several hierarchical models. The first model treated students as the first level of the hierarchy, schools as the second level, and districts as the third level. The model included a single explanatory variable, PVAAS status, at the third level of the hierarchy. We expanded this model by adding student-level variables (indicators for students who are economically disadvantaged, classified as gifted, classified as limited-English proficient, or who participated in Title 1, enrolled in the district after October 1, or enrolled in the state after October 1). The expanded model also included a school-level indicator for Title 1 status.

Another alternative model included district-level variables that differed on average between the pilot and comparison districts by more than .25 standard deviation units. For

Cohort 1, the district-level variables included the growth in average grade-5 mathematics and reading scores from 1998 to 2002, the growth in average grade-11 reading scores from 1998 to 2002, average years of experience for teachers, and the proportion of women in the district in the 2000 Census with 0 to 8 years of formal education. For Cohort 2, the difference between the pilot and comparison means differed by more than .25 standard deviation units for 15 of the over 100 variables used in matching. With 16 pilot and 16 comparison districts, controlling for 15 district-level variables would be likely to lead to unstable results for the estimated pilot program effect. Hence, we identified five of the 15 variables that were most likely to be strongly correlated with student test scores and covered the range in types of variables that differed between the pilot and comparison groups. One of these five chosen variables (average teacher salary) was not a significant predictor of test scores in any models for Cohort 2 and was deleted. The final variables included in the model were growth in average grade 5 reading scores, logarithm of the total population per square mile, percentage of women with 0 to 8 years of formal education, and the percentage of white students.

For each cohort, subject, and grade level, we also fit a final model that included student-level variables along with the school- and district-level variables.

Surveys

The survey component of this study was designed to provide information about how VAA is being used in districts and schools. We were also interested in examining how the availability of VAA data changes educators' understanding and use of information from other data sources. We estimated these effects by comparing educators in the PVAAS districts with their counterparts in the matched comparison districts, though, as we discuss in Chapter Seven, there are limitations in the extent to which these comparisons support causal conclusions.

We conducted surveys of district administrators (superintendents or other district staff responsible for making decisions from data), principals, and teachers to ascertain information about their use of data for driving educational practices and their understanding of growth modeling and value-added assessment. Educators in the PVAAS districts responded to an additional set of questions addressing their experiences with the PVAAS system and their reactions to it.

Survey Methods for Educators

This section describes the surveys administered to superintendents or central office administrators, principals, and teachers in the PVAAS and comparison districts. The goals of the survey were to contrast the practice of PVAAS and comparison district educators, to learn about the use of the value-added assessment data in the pilot districts, and to examine the context in which they are using this information.

Because so few districts were included in the PVAAS pilot program, all Cohort 1 and Cohort 2 pilot districts and the matched comparison districts were included in the sample. Two questionnaires were mailed to every superintendent in the district: one for the superintendent and one for the person in charge of the district's use of data. In our analyses, we use superintendent responses when available (53 percent of districts) and district data leader responses otherwise. The other administrators included assistant superintendents (50 percent), curriculum directors or coordinators (18 percent), assessment directors or specialists (8 percent), and other (including missing data, 24 percent).

The principal survey sample was a stratified random sample of principals from 411 schools, distributed proportionately to strata defined by district and school type (elementary or middle school) and distributed proportionately to the PVAAS and comparison districts. Data from PDE's "Education Names and Addresses" Web site (undated) provided the frame of schools with verification from the National Center for Education Statistics Common Core of Data Universe File (National Center for Education Statistics, 2006) and school district Web sites.

The teacher sample was also a stratified random sample, consisting of 2,379 teachers allocated proportionately to strata defined by district and school type. The sample was restricted to teachers who taught mathematics or English Language Arts (including reading) in grades 3 to 8. Several sources of data provided the frame of teachers, including the Pennsylvania State Education Association membership files, teacher lists from the vendor Market Data Retrieval, and lists culled from school and district Web sites. Final eligibility was verified through teacher responses. Table 2.1 provides the sample sizes by treatment and control for teachers, principals, and district administrators.

Survey questionnaires contained items on data use and testing. Many of the questionnaire items were drawn from other studies of data use in education (e.g., Hamilton et al., 2007; Dembosky et al., 2006). The items that addressed PVAAS were developed specifically for this study. The district administrator instrument was reviewed by one district superintendent as well as state officials, and was revised in response to their comments. The principal questionnaire was piloted with three principals, and the teacher questionnaire was piloted with two teachers. The full instruments are included in Appendix B.

We mailed questionnaires to all superintendents' offices in late winter of 2006. Superintendents who failed to respond to the initial mailing were sent mail and email reminders, contacted repeatedly by phone, and sent follow-up surveys. Follow-up continued through July 2006. Questionnaires were simultaneously mailed to principals at their schools. Principals who failed to respond received follow-up postcards, a second questionnaire mailing, emails

Table 2.1
Sample Sizes and Response Rates for Principals and Teachers

		Number Sampled	Number of Respondents	Simple Response Rate (%)
Principals				
PVAAS	Elementary	160	91	56.9
	Middle	59	33	55.9
Comparison	Elementary	142	85	59.9
	Middle	50	31	62.0
Teachers				
PVAAS	Elementary	830	343	41.3
	Middle	366	141	38.5
Comparison	Elementary	823	400	48.6
	Middle	360	163	45.3

with links to an online questionnaire, questionnaires sent by FedEx, and repeated phone calls. Follow-up continued through June 2006, at which time schools were closed and we could no longer reach the principals. The initial teacher questionnaire mailing also occurred in the late winter of 2006, with questionnaires sent to teachers' homes or schools. Teachers who failed to respond to the initial mailing received postcard reminders and follow-up questionnaires.

We received completed questionnaires from either superintendents or their designees in 79 out of 93 districts (85 percent).[7] Response rates were similar for the PVAAS and comparison districts (83 percent pilot, 87 percent comparison). To account for differential response rates for superintendents from districts with different values on observed characteristics, we developed nonresponse weights to adjust the responses of the administrators who completed the survey. The weights equal the reciprocal of the probability of response (Little and Rubin, 2002; Robins and Rotnitzky, 1995). They were estimated using logistic regression with forward variable selection, with variables added until the standardized bias between weighted respondents and nonrespondents was small for all available district-level variables. The variables included all the variables used in matching. In general, nonresponding districts tended to have greater proportions of African-American and Hispanic students, as well as smaller percentages of adults in the labor force or working in Pennsylvania, than responding districts. The tax efforts—the districts' tax revenue divided by property wealth in the districts—also differed between respondents and nonrespondents. However, after applying the weights, the groups were comparable.

Overall, 240 of the 411 sampled principals (58 percent) responded to our survey. Table 2.1 presents response rates by the PVAAS and comparison groups. Despite extensive follow-up efforts, the overall response rate from principals was moderately low. The low response rate increases the potential for bias from differential response. We use nonresponse weights to account for differential response rates on observable characteristics of all schools in the sample, but we cannot control for the potential for bias from unobserved variables. Principal nonresponse weights were estimated in two stages. Stage 1 calculated weights equaling the inverse of the probability of response by district and school type stratum. We calculated additional weights to account for districts with nonrespondents in a stratum of one or more school types. These weights equaled the inverse probability of a district having no respondents, as estimated by generalized boosting methods ([GBM]; McCaffrey, Ridgeway and Morral, 2004) or logistic regression using district characteristics. The models were fit within groups defined by PVAAS status (PVAAS or comparison) and school type. Stage 2 calculated weights as the inverse of estimated probabilities of individual principals responding. GBM provided the estimated probabilities within groups defined by PVAAS status and school type. The weights from the two stages were averaged. The weighted means for the respondent sample of the variables used for weighting closely matched means of the entire sample.

Table 2.1 also gives the response rates for the teachers (44 percent overall). In both the PVAAS and comparison sample, the response rates were very low. This allows for significant potential for bias from unobserved differences between the respondents and nonrespondents. We account for differential response on observable characteristics of the teachers' schools and districts through the use of nonresponse weights. Teacher nonresponse weights equal the reciprocal of the response probabilities estimated by GBM using school and district variables within

---

[7]   There are 93 total sampled districts because one district was selected as a comparison for both the Cohort 1 and Cohort 2 pilot districts. This district receives double weight in analyses that combine cohorts.

groups defined by PVAAS status and school type. The weighted means of these school and district variables very closely matched the means for the entire sample.

As discussed below, for both the principals and teacher analyses, we identified educators in the PVAAS districts who we defined as "engaged" in PVAAS. Engaged principals had seen their schools' PVAAS reports and knew their schools were participating in the pilot program. Engaged teachers had heard of PVAAS and knew their schools were participating in the program. Sixty percent of responding PVAAS principals and 23 percent of responding PVAAS teachers met these criteria. Our analyses focused on these educators and similar educators in the comparison districts. To obtain estimates for similar educators in the comparison districts, we developed weights so that the distributions of school and district variables for educators from the comparison districts matched the distributions of the variables for the engaged educators from the PVAAS districts. We used the methods of McCaffrey et al. (2004) to create and analyze the weights. Variables used in this analysis include the district variables used in matching districts as well as the following school variables: percentage of students by racial-ethnic group, percentage of low-income students, percentage of migrant students, percentage of special education students, percentage of English language learner (ELL) students, test scores in reading and mathematics from 2001 and 2002 (before PVAAS reporting), school community type (urban, suburban, or rural), average daily membership, attendance rate, full time equivalent teachers, and schoolwide Title 1 status.

The weighting succeeded in making the groups similar on most variables, but there were a few differences that remained for both principals and teachers. For principals, the variables with notable differences in the means (absolute standardized biases from .38 to .20) were

- the percentage of migrant students in the school
- the percentage of American Indian students in the school
- the percentage of English language learners in the school
- the percentage of special education students in the school
- the slopes for growth in the district's grade 5 mathematics and reading scores
- the percentage of African-American students in the school district
- the percentage of other-race students in the school district
- the average teacher tenure in the district
- the district tax effort
- the district's average instructional expense per pupil
- the percentage of Hispanics in the district population from the 2000 Census
- the percentage of adult females not in the labor force from the 2000 Census
- the median home price from the 2000 Census.

The percentage of migrant or American Indian students is generally extremely low (less than 1 percent) and the differences are small on an absolute scale. Similarly, the difference in the percentage of English language learners and special education students was just one percentage point, (2 percent ELL for engaged PVAAS versus 3 percent ELL for comparisons principals, and 10 versus 11 percent for special education). The samples match well on many test measures, and the slopes are variable and at best weakly related to current school performance. The remaining variables mostly measure district finance and community characteristics that are likely to be only weakly related the outcomes in individual schools. Hence, we have confidence that the samples are well matched on a very large number of observable characteristics.

For the teachers, the engaged teachers differed from the weighted comparison group (absolute standardized biases from .00 to .82) on

- the percentage of Asian students in the school and school district
- the percentage of American Indian students in the school
- the percentage migrant students in the school
- the average 1998 grade 5 reading score for the district
- the average 1999 grade 5 mathematics score for the district
- the average 1999 grade 8 reading score for the district
- the slope for growth in the district's grade 5 mathematics scores
- the percentage of vacant housing in the district from the 2000 Census
- the percentage of adult females not in the labor force from the 2000 Census
- the percentage of adult females with 0–8 years of education from the 2000 Census
- the median home price from the 2000 Census
- the district tax effort.

The percentages of Asian and American Indian students were generally very low for all schools, and differences were small on an absolute scale. The differences in test scores are somewhat troubling, but the groups are similar on the means of more recent test scores and many other test-score measures. The other variables with notable difference between the engaged teachers and weighted comparison teachers are mostly community variables, and are only weakly related to student achievement when other variables are taken into account; these variables do not have a clear link to teachers' use of data or likely response to PVAAS. Hence, the two groups of teachers are very similar on a large number of observed variables.

Given the modest response rates for both principals and teachers, we focus on the engaged educators who responded to our survey and the differences between these educators and educators from the comparison sample in similar schools and districts and who responded to the survey. Generalizations beyond this sample could result in incorrect inferences. We fully discuss this issue and other limitations of the analyses in Chapter Seven: Summary and Implications.

CHAPTER THREE

Effects of PVAAS on Student Achievement

The primary question that motivated this study is whether district participation in the PVAAS pilot affects student achievement. As discussed in Chapter Two, the matching of PVAAS districts with similar districts that were not participating in PVAAS provides a quasi-experimental design that can support causal inferences about PVAAS effects. This chapter summarizes the results of the achievement analysis.

Table 3.1 provides means and standard deviations of individual student-level PSSA test scores for the pilot and control districts by cohort, subject, and grade level for the 2003–2004, 2004–2005, and 2005–2006 school years. Cohort 1 school districts received their first reports in February 2003, so all years of testing occurred at least 12 months after the districts started receiving reports. Cohort 2 school districts received their first reports in the fall of 2004, which was after the first wave of testing examined here (2003–2004) and only a few months before the second wave (2004–2005). For Cohort 2 schools, only the 2005–2006 testing occurred more than a year after the districts received their PVAAS reports. If receipt of PVAAS reports spurs changes in policy or practice that lead to improved achievement, we would expect to see effects on Cohort 1 districts in all three testing waves, but only in the third wave for Cohort 2 districts.

In all comparisons across both cohorts, the effect sizes for the difference between the pilot and comparison districts, i.e., the differences in means to the standard deviation in the scores, range from less then 1 percent to about 15 percent of a standard deviation. None of the differences result in statistically significant estimates of pilot program effects in any of our models. In particular, for Cohort 2, the differences between the scores for the PVAAS and comparison districts in 2003–2004 (before testing occurred) are similar in direction and magnitude to the differences between the groups during the next two years.

As described in Chapter Two, we tested for differences between the means of the PVAAS and comparison districts using aggregated data and individual student data using hierarchical linear models. We considered alternative specifications for the hierarchical linear models, with differing combinations of student- and district-level covariates. Table 3.2 presents the Cohort 1 models with student and district variables for all three years of test scores combined. The data has been standardized within years to have a standard deviation of one, so the estimated effects for PVAAS are given as standard effect sizes. The estimated effects were somewhat sensitive to the model specification, but the signs of the estimates were stable across models for every year, subject, and grade level. Furthermore, combing the data from the all the years did not change the qualitative findings of small, statistically insignificant differences.

The estimated effects for Cohort 2 in 2004–2005 and 2005–2006 were somewhat sensitive to the models; sometimes the sign of the effect would change with the models. However,

Table 3.1
PSSA Means (Standard Deviations) by Grade Level, Year, PVAAS Cohort, and Pilot Status

	Cohort 1			Cohort 2		
	Pilot	Comparison	Effect Size Difference × 100	Pilot	Comparison	Effect Size Difference × 100
Grade 5 Mathematics						
2003–2004	1,368.2 (239.6)	1,371.2 (237.4)	−1.3	1,426.6 (230.6)	1,397.0 (236.6)	12.6
2004–2005	1,400.9 (224.2)	1,402.3 (231.5)	−0.6	1,447.7 (212.6)	1,433.0 (225.4)	6.7
2005–2006	1,405.4 (241.3)	1,405.3 (240.2)	0.0	1,455.0 (237.7)	1,445.5 (240.2)	4.0
Grade 8 Mathematics						
2003–2004	1,320.9 (206.9)	1,334.2 (208.5)	−6.4	1,381.1 (202.8)	1,369.1 (219.3)	5.7
2004–2005	1,344.1 (223.6)	1,350.4 (224.4)	−2.8	1,403.3 (226.7)	1,369.7 (218.5)	15.1
2005–2006	1,342.3 (219.3)	1,349.9 (225.7)	−3.4	1,401.3 (215.9)	1381.4 (221.3)	9.1
Grade 5 Reading						
2003–2004	1,337.6 (245.0)	1,358.5 (242.2)	−8.6	1,419.1 (231.2)	1,394.3 (245.9)	10.4
2004–2005	1,294.1 (238.8)	1,314.5 (239.3)	−8.5	1,376.2 (220.9)	1,342.5 (238.9)	14.6
2005–2006	1,273.1 (235.5)	1,292.8 (233.1)	−8.4	1,349.8 (219.1)	1333.0 (232.1)	7.4
Grade 8 Reading						
2003–2004	1,323.2 (248.0)	1,343.4 (246.2)	−8.1	1,397.3 (223.2)	1,393.1 (252.1)	1.7
2004–2005	1,306.6 (280.3)	1,325.7 (273.7)	−6.9	1,382.8 (269.0)	1,381.5 (272.4)	0.5
2005–2006	1,364.9 (279.5)	1,387.6 (285.5)	−8.0	1,458.9 (269.5)	1,454.9 (299.1)	1.4

none of the estimated effects was ever significant at the 0.05 level. For grade 8 reading, the estimated pilot program effects for models that controlled for district-level variables were large in magnitude, negative, and significant at 0.10 level in 2004–2005, but this pattern did not repeat with the 2005–2006 data. Given the general instability of the results and the potential for finding spurious results when considering estimated effects for multiple cohorts, subjects, and grade levels, we do not believe this result should be interpreted as an indication that PVAAS has negative effects on student outcomes. Rather, we conclude that the analyses of test scores provide no evidence of effects for the PVAAS pilot program.

Table 3.3 presents the models with student and district variables for 2005–2006 by subject and grade. Because only the 2005–2006 testing occurred more than a year after the

Table 3.2
Models for Cohort 1 Student Achievement by Subject and Grade, All Years of Test Data Combined

Variable	Grade 5		Grade 8	
	Mathematics	Reading	Mathematics	Reading
District Variables				
Intercept	1421.67***	1309.52***	1366.63***	1422.35***
PVAAS	0.012	−0.026	−0.039	−0.039
School Year 2003–2004[a]	−41.789***	59.464***	−14.024***	−54.884***
School Year 2004–2005[a]	−3.296***	24.337***	0.815***	−64.974***
Average teacher tenure	0.029	0.022	0.032	0.029
Grade 5 reading, time trend in PSSA score, slope	−0.004	−0.001	−0.009	−0.009
Grade 5 math, time trend in PSSA score, slope	0.012**	0.006*	0.013**	0.011*
Grade 11 math, time trend in PSSA score, slope	0.000	0.001	-0.002	-0.002
Percentage of women with 0–8 years of education	0.726	0.373	0.359	−0.306
Student Variables				
Economically disadvantaged	−0.346***	−0.378***	−0.401***	−0.428***
Gender code 0[b]	−0.367***	−0.216*	−0.431***	−0.336***
Female[b]	−0.049***	0.179***	−0.007	0.246***
Gifted	1.224***	1.07***	1.367***	1.18***
Enrolled in district after October 1 of testing year	−0.286***	−0.203***	−0.375***	−0.311***
Enrolled in state after October 1 of testing year	−0.125**	−0.148	−0.01	−0.009
Limited English proficient	−0.409***	−0.631***	−0.418***	−0.729***
Special education inside the district	−1.048***	−1.143***	−0.959***	−1.07***
Special education outside the district	−1.106***	−1.224***	−0.992***	−1.124***
Not a Title 1 school[c]	−0.097*	−0.086*	−0.169***	−0.16***
Title 1 for eligible students[c]	−0.137***	−0.098**	−0.064	−0.087
Title 1 grandfathered[c]	−0.108	−0.089		
Participating in Title 1 programs	−0.516***	−0.522***	−0.328***	−0.287***

[a] The omitted year is 2005–2006.
[b] Male is the omitted category; for a small number of records, the state data included gender coded as 0 and distinct from male or female.
[c] Whole-school Title 1 is the omitted category.
* Statistically significant, $p < .05$.
** Statistically significant, $p < 0.01$.
*** Statistically significant, $p < 0.001$.

Table 3.3
Models for Cohort 2 Student Achievement by Subject and Grade, 2005–2006 Test Data

Variable	Grade 5		Grade 8	
District Variables				
Intercept	1421.87***	1310.01***	1366.89***	0.147***
PVAAS	0.069	0.034	0.015	−0.06
Average teacher tenure	0.03	0.006	0.019	0.008
Grade 5 reading, time trend in PSSA score, slope	−0.015	−0.006	−0.017**	−0.016*
Grade 5 Math, time trend in PSSA score, slope	0.002	0.008	0.015*	0.018*
Grade 11 math, time Trend in PSSA score, slope	0.007	0.007	0.004	0.002
Percentage of women with 0–8 years of education	−6.603*	−5.923*	−3.412	−5.007*
Student Variables				
Economically disadvantaged	−0.334***	−0.387***	−0.425***	−0.444***
Gender code 0[a]	0.164	−0.158	0.277	−0.065
Female[a]	−0.107***	0.158***	−0.028	0.229***
Gifted	1.35***	0.971***	1.284***	1.133***
Enrolled in district after October 1 of testing year	−0.339***	−0.332***	−0.532***	−0.522***
Enrolled in state after October 1 of testing year	−0.15	0.009	−0.042	0.157
Limited English proficient	−0.387***	−0.497***	−0.676***	−1.029***
Special education inside the district	−1.703***	−2.04***	−0.406	−0.039
Special education outside the district	−1.299***	−1.192***		
Participating in Title 1 programs	−0.593***	−0.584***	0.005***	−0.054

[a] Male is the omitted category; for a small number of records, the state data included gender coded as 0 and distinct from male or female.

* Satistically significant, $p < .05$.

** Statistically significant, $p < 0.01$.

*** Statistically significant, $p < 0.001$.

Cohort 2 PVAAS districts received their first PVAAS reports, we present only the models for this year of testing.

The analyses of test scores consider students' average achievement but do not consider student progress or growth. Provided the matching removes any preexisting difference between the PVAAS and comparison districts, the analysis of achievement yields estimates of the causal effects of the PVAAS program. However, because PVAAS focuses on student growth, measures of growth might provide a more precise measure. The Pennsylvania State Department of Education could not provide us with longitudinal data for individual students, so we did not look at growth for individual students. However, SAS, which developed the PVAAS methodology and oversees the creation of the PVAAS reports, conducted its own analysis using cumulative growth measures. These unpublished analyses found that growth was greater in the PVAAS sample than in a comparison sample, although the difference was not significant, and that, overall, students in 81 percent of the PVAAS districts had positive cumulative growth in the aggregate, compared to just 58 percent of students in the comparison districts. Given the small sample size, the p-value of a test of the significance of this difference is 0.054.[1]

Summary

Overall differences in average achievement between the PVAAS and the comparison districts are very small and never statistically significant, regardless of the models used to test the differences. There are a few limitations to keep in mind when interpreting these results. The numbers of districts in each cohort are small, and this could result in insufficient statistical power to detect effects. Furthermore, the limited time available for the PVAAS program to affect educators or student outcomes should be taken into consideration when interpreting these results; educational interventions often require several years to take hold and lead to improved achievement (Borman et al., 2002; Gill et al., 2005).

It is difficult to interpret these comparisons without knowing something about how educators have responded to the provision of PVAAS information. The next three chapters summarize results from analyses of data on the survey responses of superintendents, principals, and teachers.

---

[1]   The results of SAS's study are not published and we were unable to obtain the methodological details of this study. However, we did receive the aggregate district-level data and were able to replicate the analyses. We do not have disaggregated data or information on how the aggregated data were generated.

CHAPTER FOUR

Superintendents' Responses to PVAAS

In this chapter, we present the results from the superintendent surveys. We begin with a comparison of PVAAS and non-PVAAS districts to a set of questions about data use. The second part of this chapter examines the responses of PVAAS participants to a set of questions about their understanding and use of the PVAAS program and the reports it generates. Because the pilot included only a relatively small sample of districts, the analyses have only limited power to detect differences between PVAAS and comparison district administrators. For PVAAS to affect student outcomes would probably require fairly substantial changes in actions and opinions of administrators and other educators, so a focus on large effects might be warranted. But the inability of these analyses to detect small or even some moderate effects should be kept in mind.

Actions and Opinions in PVAAS and Comparison Districts

We compared the two groups on several sets of questions addressing use of achievement data, opinions about test-based accountability, and perceived facilitators and barriers to effective data use. Each set of results is presented below.

Use of Achievement Data

The first set of questions explored district leaders' perceptions of the utility of several sources of data. A primary rationale for providing educators with access to VAA information is that it will lead to improved student outcomes by improving decisionmaking. One of the challenges in promoting effective data use in education, however, is that administrators and teachers are often overwhelmed with data from various sources (Marsh, Pane, and Hamilton, 2006). Receiving many types of data could have positive or negative effects on educators' ability to use the data effectively, depending in part on whether they are able to distinguish among sources that are more or less useful for informing the decisions they need to make.

Table 4.1 summarizes the responses of PVAAS and non-PVAAS administrators to a series of questions addressing the perceived utility of test-score data for improving student performance in the district. Superintendents in the two groups had similar views. In each group, the majority of administrators found scores on the state's PSSA tests very useful, especially when disaggregated by schools, special populations, or topics or skills. The state has developed several relationships with vendors to analyze and report performance on PSSA and other measures, but few administrators in either group found this information (reports from Standard and Poor's schoolmatters.com Web site and the Grow Network, and eMetric's online tool) very

Table 4.1
Administrators' Views on the Usefulness of Various Sources of Information for Improving Student Performance

Source of Information	Percentage of Administrators Who Reported That the Information Is Very Useful	
	Pilot Districts (n=39)	Comparison Districts (n=40)
Scores on the PSSA or district standardized tests for the district as a whole	68	57
Scores on the PSSA or district standardized tests for each school in the district	70	63
Schoolwide results on the PSSA or district standardized tests summarized for each student subgroup (e.g., special education, race/ethnicity, economically disadvantaged)	63	65
Schoolwide results on the PSSA or district standardized tests broken down by topic or skill	73	77
Student performance on interim or diagnostic assessments (e.g., DIBELS, DRA, or district-developed interim assessments)	73	62
Reports of individual student *growth* in achievement from one year to the next on any achievement test[a]	**61**	**27**
Analysis or reports provided by a data team (i.e., a team of teachers and/or administrators tasked with analyzing and summarizing student achievement test results)	73	64
Information from the Standard and Poor's reports (schoolmatters.com)	18	11
Reports from the Grow Network	48	32
Information from the PSSA eMetric tool[b]	31	32

NOTES: Statistically significant differences are indicated by bold typeface ($p < 0.05$). Response options were (1) Not available or haven't heard of this, (2) Not useful, (3) Minimally useful, (4) Moderately useful, and (5) Very useful. DIBELS = Dynamic Indicators of Basic Early Literacy Skills, DRA = Developmental Reading Assessment.

[a] Due to item nonresponse, n=39 comparison district administrators for this item.

[b] Due to item nonresponse, n=38 PVAAS district administrators for this item.

useful.[1] The only large and statistically significant difference between the groups concerns their evaluation of the utility of reports on student growth. The majority (61 percent) of administrators from the pilot districts reported that such information is "very useful" for improving performance, compared to just 21 percent of the administrators in the comparison districts. PVAAS has made growth data available to administrators who would otherwise not have had access to it (as discussed below, growth data of any kind were reported to be unavailable to 30 percent of comparison districts), and many found this information useful.

We also considered the perceived utility among administrators who reported that the source of information is available and that they had seen it. Because the vast majority of administrators reported access to each type of information, restricting the sample has no appreciable effect on most results. The one exception is reports on individual student growth. As would be

---

[1]   eMetric is an interactive, Web-based PSSA analysis tool. Standard and Poor's and the Grow Network have contracts with Pennsylvania to provide specialized reporting of test scores and other data.

expected, more administrators from PVAAS districts reported having access to growth data. Ninety-four percent of the administrators from the PVAAS districts reported having seen such reports, compared to only 70 percent of the administrators in the comparison districts.[2] This difference is statistically significant (p < 0.01). We do not have information on the source of growth data provided to comparison districts. Among the administrators with access to growth data, 66 percent of those from PVAAS districts reported that the data are very useful, but only 39 percent from comparison districts found the reports very useful. Again, the difference is significant (p < 0.05). The difference in utility might result from the extra training provided to the PVAAS districts or the high quality of the PVAAS reports.

In addition to understanding respondents' perceptions of the utility of different data sources, it is important to examine how administrators use these data. Table 4.2 compares the extent to which respondents in both groups reported using results from state and district achievement tests to make various decisions. There are no significant differences between the two groups, and for most purposes the responses are very similar. The largest differences are

Table 4.2
Administrators' Use of the State and District Achievement Test Results for Various Purposes in 2004–2005 and 2005–2006

Purpose	Percentage of Administrators Who Reported Moderate or Extensive Use of Results for This Purpose	
	PVAAS Pilot Districts (n=39)	Comparison Districts (n=40)
Make changes to the district's curriculum and instructional materials	93	86
Develop a district improvement plan	81	71
Help individual schools develop school improvement plans	82	69
Make policy about how much time is spent on each academic subject	51	53
Assign or reassign staff	41	26
Monitor schools' implementation of curricula or use of resources	77	75
Focus principal and/or teacher professional development	93	83
Make decisions about budget or resource allocation	77	78
Evaluate the effectiveness of specific programs	85	82
Evaluate principal or teacher performance	29	39
Reward school staff for achieving strong performance (e.g., bonuses, awards)	22	23
Adjust the level of authority principals have over school decisions (e.g., curriculum, schedule, budget)[a]	19	28
Communicate with parents or other community members	84	79

NOTES: None of the differences between pilot and comparison districts is statistically significant (p < 0.05). Response options were (1) Did not use in this way, (2) Used minimally, (3) Used moderately, and (4) Used extensively.

[a] Due to item nonresponse, n=38 PVAAS district administrators for this item.

---

[2]   Note that individual growth reports are not restricted to the PVAAS reports and could be accessible to administrators from both districts.

for reassigning staff (reported to be used moderately or extensively in 41 percent of pilot versus 26 percent of comparison districts) and helping individual schools develop improvement plans (reported to be used moderately or extensively in 82 percent of pilot versus 69 percent of comparison districts), but neither of these differences is statistically significant given the modest sample sizes. Generally, the vast majority of administrators reported using test results to make changes to curriculum and instructional materials; to plan, monitor, and evaluate programs and the budget; to focus professional development; and to communicate with parents or community members. Few administrators reported using test-score data to make decisions regarding staff, such as determining assignments, awarding bonuses, or evaluating performance.

Support for Test-Based Accountability

One measure of support for the idea of data-driven decisionmaking is administrators' opinions about the state accountability system enacted in response to NCLB. The provision of PVAAS information could change the level of enthusiasm for testing and accountability, conceivably in either direction. As shown in Table 4.3, however, there are no significant differences between

Table 4.3
Administrators' Opinions About the State's Accountability System Under NCLB, Including PSSA Testing and Designation of AYP Status

Statement	Percentage of Administrators Who Agreed or Strongly Agreed	
	Pilot Districts (n=38)	Comparison Districts (n=40)
Overall, the state's NCLB accountability system has been beneficial for students in my district.[a]	76	61
The state's NCLB accountability system leaves little time to teach content not on the PSSA.	47	50
As a result of the state's NCLB accountability system, high-achieving students are not receiving appropriately challenging curriculum or instruction.[b]	31	27
We have made substantial changes in the district's curriculum to improve student performance on the PSSA.	77	78
PSSA scores accurately reflect the achievement of students in my district.[a]	62	46
Our district's AYP status accurately reflects the overall performance of my district.	47	45
AYP status generally provides an accurate picture of individual school performance for schools in my district.	37	43
Differences in student characteristics from year to year make it difficult for my schools and district to make AYP.	42	49
Because of pressure to meet the AYP target, my staff and I are focusing more on improving student achievement than we would without the AYP target.	62	67
The state's NCLB accountability system does not adequately consider student growth.	80	73

NOTES: None of the differences between pilot and comparison districts is statistically significant (p < 0.05). Response options were (1) Strongly disagree, (2) Disagree, (3) Agree, and (4) Strongly agree.

[a] Due to item nonresponse, n=37 PVAAS and n=39 pilot district administrators for this item.

[b] Due to item nonresponse, n=36 PVAAS district administrators for this item.

administrators from the pilot and the comparison districts in their responses to several questions about the state accountability system. Administrators from the pilot districts were more likely to report that the state's NCLB accountability system is beneficial for their students (76 percent versus 61 percent) and more likely to believe the state's PSSA test accurately reflects the achievement of their students (62 percent versus 46 percent). All other differences tend to be very small. A large majority of administrators in both groups agreed that they made substantial changes in curriculum to improve PSSA scores. Similarly, large majorities of administrators in both groups agreed with statements that NCLB does not adequately consider growth and that Adequate Yearly Progress (AYP) is increasing the focus on student achievement. There was less agreement with statements about possible negative consequences of an accountability system, such as NCLB restricting time for subjects not tested, or curriculum not meeting the needs of high-achieving students. There was also limited support for statements about AYP providing accurate measures of the schools or school district. It appears that district leaders, whether or not they have participated in PVAAS, recognize the limited value of the AYP designation.

Facilitators and Barriers

Actions taken at the district level may facilitate or hinder the use of data by principals and teachers. The next set of results compares PVAAS and non-PVAAS district administrators' reports of assistance provided to schools. The first set of questions explores resources related to data use generally (Table 4.4). It is followed by a set of questions examining support for test-preparation activities (Table 4.5). The former are likely to be considered generally beneficial,

Table 4.4
Administrators' Provision of Various Types of Support in Using and Analyzing Data in 2004–2005 and 2005–2006

Type of Support	Percentage of Administrators Who Reported Providing This Type of Support to Some of Their Schools	
	Pilot Districts (n=39)	Comparison Districts (n=40)
Purchased computer software or systems for re-analyzing test results	53	52
Provided staff to assist schools with data analysis or perform additional analyses	81	64
Provided staff to work with particular schools to make instructional changes based on data analyses	70	72
Provided professional development to *principals* to help them use and analyze data[a]	91	84
Provided professional development to *teachers* to help them use and analyze data	95	89
Helped schools prepare complete and accurate data to comply with NCLB reporting requirements	93	90

NOTES: None of the differences between pilot and comparison districts is statistically significant ($p < 0.05$). Response options were (1) No schools, (2) Low-performing schools only, (3) High-performing schools only, (4) Some low- and some high-performing schools, and (5) All schools. Table cells indicate percentages with responses 2 through 5.
[a] Due to item nonresponse, n=38 PVAAS district administrators for this item.

whereas the latter raise concerns about narrowing of curriculum and instruction and other potentially harmful effects of high-stakes testing.

Among most of the data use questions, the vast majority of administrators in both groups reported providing resources to help schools analyze and interpret data, including additional staff and professional development. One exception is computers or software for running analyses, which were provided by only about half of the districts. Although there are no statistically significant differences between the groups, administrators from PVAAS districts were more likely to report providing staff to support data analysis and providing professional development on data analysis to principals and teachers. This increased emphasis on data analysis by principals and teachers is consistent with goals of PVAAS to promote the use of data.

Another way in which administrators might respond to testing and the provision of test-score data is through efforts to improve student achievement on those tests (as opposed to improving student learning more generally). Table 4.5 shows that large majorities of administrators in both groups reported engaging in test-preparation activities. Nearly all districts gave their teachers materials to help students practice for the test, such as commercial test-preparation materials and released copies of the PSSA test, and nearly all aimed to familiarize teachers with the content of the test by helping them identify content likely to be on the PSSA and discussing the state Assessment Anchors[3] with teachers. A lesser majority of districts went even further and actively encouraged teachers to spend more time on tested subjects and less time on other subjects, and 70 percent of districts encouraged staff to focus on students who are close to meeting standards. These practices, which have the potential to inflate test scores (Koretz and Hamilton, 2006), occurred with similar frequencies in both groups.

Table 4.5
Administrators' Efforts to Help Teachers Prepare Students for the PSSA

Activity	Percentage of Administrators Who Reported Engaging in the Activity	
	Pilot Districts (n=39)	Comparison Districts (n=40)
Distributed commercial test-preparation materials (e.g., practice tests)	85	81
Distributed released copies of the PSSA test or items	82	96
Discussed methods for preparing students for the PSSA at staff meetings	96	100
Encouraged or required school staff to spend more time on tested subjects and less time on other subjects	62	59
Helped school staff identify content that is likely to appear on the PSSA so they can cover it adequately in their instruction	94	100
Encouraged school staff to focus on students *close* to meeting standards (e.g., close to proficient)	70	70
Discussed the state's Assessment Anchors with school staff	96	100

NOTES: None of the differences between pilot and comparison districts is statistically significant (p < 0.05). Response options were (1) Yes and (2) No.

---

[3] To supplement the Pennsylvania Academic Standards, in 2004–2005 the state produced a set of Assessment Anchors (now called Assessment Anchor Content Standards), for grades 3 through 8 and 11 in mathematics and reading. These anchors are intended to clarify which standards are going to be assessed at which grade levels on the PSSA.

The extent to which districts promote data use might be affected by the support and resources they receive from the state or intermediate unit. We asked respondents to indicate whether each of several resources is available to them, and in cases where it is available, how useful it is for making decisions about district improvement. Interestingly, pilot districts reported having less access to these resources than comparison districts (Table 4.6). For districts that have access, the usefulness ratings by pilot and comparison districts were similar. The exception is for technical assistance with data analysis: Pilot district administrators were more likely than their counterparts to rate this assistance as useful. Although we do not have information about the nature of this technical assistance, it is likely that many PVAAS districts received assistance specifically tailored to the PVAAS reporting system, and this intervention might explain some of the difference in perceived usefulness.

District capacity to promote data use may also be hindered by a number of factors. As shown in Table 4.7, the most commonly reported hindrances involved time: receiving test scores late in the year and lacking time for careful examination of scores. For both of these factors, administrators in pilot districts were somewhat more likely to report the factor as a problem, but the differences are not significant. Administrators in pilot districts were significantly more likely (29 percent versus 9 percent) to report lack of technology as a hindrance to using test-score data, although this was a relatively uncommon problem in both groups. This difference might stem in part from the technology required to use the PVAAS reporting system. The administrators in pilot districts were also significantly less likely to report that lack of access to growth data was a hindrance (20 percent versus 41 percent). Clearly, the PVAAS reports address a perceived need. However, it is surprising that 20 percent of the administrators in the pilot districts reported a lack of growth data that limits their use of test scores. In Ohio, where

Table 4.6
Administrators' Views on the Usefulness of Various Resources for Making Decisions on District Improvement

Resource	Percentage of Administrators Who Reported That the Resource Was Provided		Of Those Who Reported That the Resource Was Available, the Percentage of Who Reported That It Was Moderately or Very Useful	
	Pilot Districts (n=39)	Comparison Districts (n=38)	Pilot Districts	Comparison Districts
Workshops or meetings where test results are presented and explained	77	87	81	72
Training on how to use test results for instructional planning or district improvement	82	96	75	71
Information on available data analysis systems and/or guidance on selecting these systems	**74**	**98**	71	69
Technical assistance with data analysis[a]	86	87	**74**	**54**
Technical assistance with technology[a]	79	89	63	58

NOTES: Statistically significant differences are indicated by bold typeface (p < 0.05). Response options were (1) Not provided, (2) Not useful, (3) Minimally useful, (4) Moderately useful, and (5) Very useful. The denominator for the percentage reporting usefulness was the number of administrators who reported that the resources were provided, that is, who responded with options 2 through 5.

[a] Due to item nonresponse, n=38 PVAAS district administrators for this item.

Table 4.7
Administrators' Views on Whether Various Factors Hinder the Effective Use of State and District Achievement Data

Factor Affecting Data Use	Percentage of Administrators Who Reported That the Factor Moderately or Greatly Hinders Effective Use of Data	
	Pilot Districts (n=39)	Comparison Districts (n=40)
Lack of access to achievement results for students currently enrolled in this district	30	28
Difficult-to-understand reports or displays of achievement results	24	16
Insufficient technology (e.g., computers, software, high-speed Internet connection)	**29**	**9**
Lack of staff to address technology problems	27	33
Lack of district central office staff skilled in data analysis and interpretation	26	33
Insufficient time to examine and interpret results carefully[a]	71	59
Receiving test results late in the year	92	77
Teachers' and/or principals' lack of skills or experience with analyzing data	39	45
Lack of access to information about student growth in achievement[b]	**20**	**41**

NOTES: Statistically significant differences are indicated by bold typeface (p < 0.05). Response options were (1) Not a hindrance, (2) Slight hindrance, (3) Moderate hindrance, and (4) Great hindrance.

[a] Due to item nonresponse, n=39 comparison district administrators for this item.

[b] Due to item nonresponse, n=38 PVAAS district administrators for this item.

administrators received similar value-added reports, some administrators dismissed estimates with large standard errors as being too unreliable to be useful, and this might explain part of the response from the PVAAS pilots. Also, given that growth data are generally not available to administrators in the comparison districts, it is interesting that only 41 percent of these administrators viewed the lack of growth data as a hindrance. We cannot determine from these results whether these administrators have access to growth data from sources other than PVAAS, or whether they do not view such data as important for decisionmaking.

Effective use of growth measures requires an understanding of how they differ from other measures of student achievement and the extent to which they are influenced by factors under the control of schools. The provision of information about individual student growth is relatively new in Pennsylvania, and it is possible that exposure to this information and the resources that accompany it might affect district administrators' understanding of growth measures. In addition, the PVAAS training materials contain an extended discussion of growth and emphasize the limitations of level scores (because they are strongly influenced by factors outside the control of schools). We examined administrators' responses to a series of statements about growth measures. The results are presented in Table 4.8. Overall, the administrators in the PVAAS districts tended to agree or strongly agree with statements that accurately characterize growth data and were less likely to agree or strongly agree with statements that mischaracterize growth data. The differences are generally small and none are statistically significant, but the general trend suggests that the PVAAS district administrators might be better informed about

Table 4.8
Administrators' Views About Student Achievement Growth on State and District Standardized Tests

Statement	Percentage of Administrators Who Agreed or Strongly Agreed	
	Pilot Districts (n=39)	Comparison Districts (n=40)
The growth that students attain each year is strongly related to their overall intelligence.[a]	30	43
The poverty level or family circumstances of students are more important than teacher effectiveness for determining student growth.	12	23
Teachers have a significant influence on the progress students make in their achievement each year.	98	92
A year of exposure to an ineffective teacher can affect students' performance in future school year.	100	94
School-level changes in average test scores are good indicators of whether *students* in those schools have achieved growth.[b]	47	59
A school cannot meet its performance expectations under NCLB if its students' scores are declining over time.	79	86

NOTES: None of the differences between pilot and comparison districts are statistically significant (p < 0.05). Response options were (1) Strongly disagree, (2) Disagree, (3) Agree, and (4) Strongly agree. The classification of the six items according to accuracy are ambiguous, inaccurate, accurate, accurate, inaccurate, and inaccurate.

[a] Due to item nonresponse, n=39 comparison district administrators for this item.

[b] Due to item nonresponse, n=38 PVAAS district administrators for this item.

growth than their counterparts. However, sizable numbers (47 percent of pilot administrators and 59 percent of comparison administrators) appear to lack a full understanding of the difference between status and growth measures, as evidenced by agreement with the statement that school-level changes in average test scores are good indicators of individual student growth. And large majorities of administrators in both groups also agreed with the potentially incorrect statement that schools cannot meet the NCLB performance expectations if scores are declining over time.[4] Administrators in both groups were clearer on the generally accepted notions that schools and teachers affect student growth: Majorities in both groups disagreed with statements that growth is strongly affected by intelligence and that student background is a more important influence on growth than teacher effectiveness. Nearly all endorsed the view that teachers have important, lasting effects.

In sum, the results presented thus far in this chapter provide little evidence that PVAAS has influenced district administrators' actions or opinions related to testing and data use. Given the limited power of the analysis, small differences might be undetected, but overall the groups are very similar on many items, suggesting little effect associated with PVAAS. The next section examines responses of pilot district administrators to questions about actions and opinions related specifically to the PVAAS program.

---

4   Average scores could decline even as percentage proficient increased. In high-performing schools, even the percentage proficient could decrease while schools continue to meet AYP targets, particularly if score declines occur among students performing at the advanced level. The inclusion of subgroup targets creates additional complications and further reduces the link between changes in average scores and AYP status.

Responses to PVAAS Among Participating Districts

Districts must embrace and use the information from value-added analyses for the data to affect student outcomes, but to date there is very little evidence of how such information is interpreted and used. This section aims to shed light on administrators' views of PVAAS and their efforts to use the information for decisionmaking. The results reported in this section were obtained from survey items administered only to administrators in pilot districts.[5] The first set of results examines responses and opinions about the PVAAS program, and the second set focuses specifically on PVAAS reports.

Responses to the PVAAS Program

We begin with a series of questions examining administrators' opinions about PVAAS (Table 4.9). Their opinions were generally quite favorable. A large majority (80 percent) agreed that it provides accurate information about how the district is improving student achievement, a number that is in stark contrast to the 43 percent who agreed that AYP provided accurate information about their district's performance (see Table 4.3). Similarly large majorities agreed that it helps communication with parents and helps school staff see their efforts pay off. Despite the fact that the state's accountability system under NCLB focuses on proficiency rates rather than growth all along the score scale, administrators generally did not believe that PVAAS creates goals that conflict with other accountability measures. At the same time, 60 percent reported that at least some schools in their districts look better with the PVAAS measure than they do using AYP status, so there is clearly a recognition that these sources of information can lead to different conclusions about how schools are doing.

These results also suggest that administrators view PVAAS as influencing their districts and schools. Majorities agreed that PVAAS has eliminated excuses for poor performance and has led to changes in their own behavior and the behavior of educators in their schools. Only about a quarter of respondents agreed that PVAAS is *not* a good measure of students' progress toward the state standards, and even fewer expressed uncertainty about how to interpret the PVAAS school effects. Three-fourths of respondents recognized the importance of support from local teachers' associations.

Despite these generally favorable opinions, actual use of PVAAS is not as widespread as might be expected. As discussed above, only 90 percent of administrators reported seeing their district's PVAAS reports, though it is possible that some superintendents delegated the task of reviewing the reports to others in their districts. Access to PVAAS by other staff is also limited. For instance, although 80 percent of administrators reported that the PVAAS reports help school staff, only about 70 percent of administrators reported giving teachers in their districts access to the PVAAS reports. About 17 percent shared access with only teacher leaders, and only about a quarter of administrators provided access to all their teachers. Nearly all districts gave access to all principals.

When asked about specific uses of PVAAS information, only a minority of administrators reported using PVAAS moderately or extensively for each purpose (see Table 4.10). Fewer than 20 percent reported using PVAAS for setting policies about time allotment, assigning staff,

---

[5]   One administrator from a pilot district answered "no" to a screening question about whether the district participated in PVAAS. This administrator did not respond to the PVAAS-specific survey questions and is excluded from the results reported in this section.

Table 4.9
Pilot District Administrators' Opinions About PVAAS

Statement	Percentage of Pilot District Administrators (n=38) Who Agreed or Strongly Agreed
PVAAS provides an accurate indication of how well our district is improving student achievement.	80
I have made changes to my approach to managing the district in response to information from PVAAS.	64
PVAAS is discussed frequently among central office staff in this district.	51
PVAAS is not a very good measure of our students' progress toward meeting state standards.	23
PVAAS helps educators communicate more effectively with parents about their children's progress than they could without PVAAS.	81
PVAAS has caused schools in this district to increase their focus on low-performing students.	66
I am not sure I understand how to interpret the PVAAS school effects.	19
The information on student growth in PVAAS helps school staff because they can see their efforts paying off.	80
I am confident in my ability to explain conceptually (not necessarily mathematically) how a school's mean predicted score is calculated.	64
The district focuses more on the needs of high-achieving students because of PVAAS than we would without the information from PVAAS.	34
Because PVAAS focuses on growth and the state's accountability system focuses on proficiency levels, school and district staff sometimes feel like they are forced to meet conflicting goals.	36
The performance of at least some schools in this district looks better when evaluated according to growth on PVAAS rather than according to AYP status.[a]	60
The information the district receives from PVAAS is more useful for instructional planning than the information we receive from other sources.[b]	39
PVAAS eliminates excuses for poor performance because it evaluates growth.	75
Support from the local teachers' association is critical to the success of PVAAS.	76

NOTE: Response options were (1) Strongly disagree, (2) Disagree, (3) Agree, (4) Strongly agree, and (9) Don't know.

[a] Due to item nonresponse, n=36 PVAAS district administrators for this item.

[b] Due to item nonresponse, n=37 PVAAS district administrators for this item.

evaluating staff, rewarding staff, making budgeting decisions, or allocating authority to principals. Many of these results are not surprising because the activities, such as rewarding staff, are clearly outside the intended purposes advertised for PVAAS. Only 17 percent reported using PVAAS moderately or extensively to communicate with parents or the community,[6] which stands in stark contrast to the 81 percent who reported that PVAAS helps in communicating with parents (Table 4.9). This difference suggests that administrators' opinions about the utility of PVAAS for specific purposes are not based solely on their own use of the information for those purposes. PVAAS is most widely used for making curricular and professional develop-

---

[6] An additional 34 percent reported they used it minimally for this purpose.

ment decisions and improvement planning, but even for these activities administrators in only about half the districts reported moderate or extensive use.

Table 4.10 also repeats information from Table 4.2, showing PVAAS district administrators' responses to parallel items about the use of state and district achievement tests in general. Reported use is substantially lower for PVAAS than for these other tests. For example, between 75 and 95 percent of districts use state tests for various purposes (to make changes to the district's curriculum and instructional materials, develop a district improvement plan, help individual schools develop school improvement plans, monitor schools' implementation of curricula or use of resources, focus principal and/or teacher professional development, make decisions about budget or resource allocation, evaluate the effectiveness of specific programs, and communicate with parents or other community members), but no more than about 50

Table 4.10
Pilot District Administrators' Use of PVAAS Versus State or District Test Results for Various Purposes

Purpose	Percentage of Pilot District Administrators (n=33) Who Reported Moderate or Extensive Use of PVAAS Data for This Purpose	Percentage of Pilot District Administrators (n=39) Who Reported Moderate or Extensive Use of State or District Test Results for This Purpose
Make changes to the district's curriculum and instructional materials	51	93
Develop a district improvement plan	40	81
Help individual schools develop school improvement plans	46	82
Make policy about how much time is spent on each academic subject	17	51
Assign or reassign staff	9	41
Monitor schools' implementation of curricula or use of resources	27	77
Focus principal and/or teacher professional development[b]	50	93
Make decisions about budget or resource allocation	17	77
Evaluate the effectiveness of specific programs	38	85
Evaluate principal or teacher performance	12	29
Reward school staff for achieving strong performance (e.g., bonuses, awards)	11	22
Adjust the level of authority principals have over school decisions (e.g., curriculum, schedule, budget)[c]	16	19
Communicate with parents or other community members[b]	17	84

NOTE: Response options were (1) Did not use in this way, (2) Used minimally, (3) Used moderately, and (4) Used extensively.

[a] Five district administrators did not see their district's PVAAS reports and skipped these items. One additional district administrator who did see the reports skipped these items.

[b] Due to item nonresponse, n=32 PVAAS district administrators for this item about PVAAS.

[c] Due to item nonresponse, n=38 PVAAS district administrators for this item about state and district test results.

percent use PVAAS for each of these purposes. Generally, the tasks for which state and district tests were used moderately or extensively by the greatest proportion of districts were also the tasks for which PVAAS was more likely to be used moderately or extensively. The exception is communicating with parents, for which state and district test results were used extensively but PVAAS is used relatively little.

As described in Chapter One, the PVAAS reports include a variety of components. In addition to asking about how PVAAS was used, we asked administrators about their access to each report component and about its perceived usefulness (the results are shown in Table 4.11). Nearly all administrators reported seeing each core component of the PVAAS report (the first six items in Table 4.11), and most of those who saw any particular component found it moderately or very useful. Approximately half of the districts have created custom reports of any type, and only about 36 percent created teacher-level reports.[7] Few administrators accessed the hints feature of PVAAS, but those who did tended to find it useful.

The effects of PVAAS on administrators' practices depend not only on access, but also on perceived utility. Therefore, we also asked administrators their opinions about the reports (the results are shown in Table 4.12). In general, those opinions were positive. A large majority found the reports clear and the online system easy to navigate. Few found the reports redun-

Table 4.11
Pilot District Administrators' Reporting of Whether They Saw Various PVAAS Report Components and Whether They Found Them Useful

PVAAS Report Component	Percentage of Pilot District Administrators (n=34) Who Reported Seeing the Component	Of Those Who Saw the Component, the Percentage Who Reported That It Was Moderately or Very Useful
School-level reports for the schools in my district (table form)	97	73
Graphs showing growth among students in different quintiles (part of the school-level diagnostic reports)	94	74
Graphs showing growth among students in the advanced, proficient, etc., categories (part of the school-level diagnostic reports)	94	77
Subgroup reports (results disaggregated by race/ethnicity, socioeconomic status, etc.)	97	68
Student-level reports of past performance	97	76
Student-level projections of future performance	95	79
Custom reports prepared by district staff[a]	56	77
Summary reports for individual teachers[b]	36	66
The "hints" feature on the PVAAS reporting Web site[a]	31	82

NOTE: Response options were (1) I have not seen this (1), (2) Not useful, (3) Minimally useful, (4) Moderately useful, and (5) Very useful (5). The denominator used to calculate the percentage reporting moderately to very useful is the number of administrators who reported seeing the component, that is, who responded with options 2 through 5.

[a] Due to item nonresponse, n=32 PVAAS district administrators for this item.

[b] Due to item nonresponse, n=33 PVAAS district administrators for this item.

---

7 The PVAAS system does not provide teacher-level reports. These would need to be created by collecting student-level data from PVAAS and aggregating in another software system.

**Table 4.12
Administrators' Opinions About PVAAS Reports**

Statement	Percentage of Pilot District Administrators (n=33) Who Agreed or Strongly Agreed
The PVAAS reports are clear and easy to understand.	74
I refer to the PVAAS reports frequently throughout the year when planning my district improvement efforts.	54
I receive so many different reports on student achievement that I find it hard to figure out which reports to focus on.	47
PVAAS school-level diagnostic reports provide essentially the same information as the PSSA school-level reports we receive from the state.[a]	13
It is easy to navigate the PVAAS online reports.[a]	83
PVAAS reports are not helpful because they do not provide prescriptive or diagnostic information to help us figure out how to address problems.[a]	18
The PVAAS reports are available early enough in the school year to be useful.	40
Lack of alignment among the different tests used in PVAAS makes it difficult to interpret growth.	58

NOTES: Response options were (1) Strongly disagree, (2) Disagree, (3) Agree, (4) Strongly agree, and (9) Don't know.

[a] Due to item nonresponse, n=32 PVAAS district administrators for this item.

dant with other sources or rated them as unhelpful because of a lack of prescriptive information. Fewer than half found that the abundance of reports makes it hard to determine where to focus. Timing seems to be the biggest problem: Only 40 percent agreed that the reports are provided early enough to be useful. Test alignment also appears to be a problem, and this might be referring to the combining of state and district tests used to create PVAAS reports, which resulted in the complex test-pooling sample and the complex methods statistical methods used to estimate the value-added effects. State PVAAS coordinators told us that administrators considered the regression methods used to account for combining different tests to be confusing.

The utility of the PVAAS reports might be affected by users' understanding of the methods used to produce the information the reports contain. We asked several questions intended to gauge understanding of these methods. Table 4.13 indicates the percent of administrators who agreed with each statement and the percent who reported "I don't know." About half of respondents reported that they understand that the designation "NDD" is intended to signify a year's worth of growth.[8] Only about a quarter of respondents confused the PVAAS growth measure with a cohort-to-cohort change measure, and most understood that the PVAAS measures growth relative to other students.

Administrators' understanding of PVAAS is driven in part by their access to training and resources. Table 4.14 summarizes responses to questions about a set of resources the state pro-

---

[8]   NDD means *no statistically detectable difference from zero*, and the estimates are scaled so that zero means a school's students made average growth. Formally, NDD means it is not possible to distinguish between making a year's growth or making more or less than a year's growth. A response of "Disagree" could indicate a more nuanced understanding of the NDD designation.

Table 4.13
Pilot District Administrators' Understanding of the Methods Used to Produce the Information in PVAAS Reports

Statement	Percentage of Pilot District Administrators Who Agreed	Percentage of Pilot District Administrators Who Answered "I Don't Know"
A school that is assigned a PVAAS school effect of NDD (no detectable difference) has achieved a year's worth of growth in student achievement.	49	15
The PVAAS school effect for grade 5 provides an indication of school effectiveness for all tested grades up to and including grade 5.[a]	35	20
A negative PVAAS school effect for grade 5 indicates that 5th graders this year scored lower on average than 5th graders last year.	23	8
PVAAS measures of individual student growth depend not only on the student's current and previous scores but on the scores attained by other students.	63	11

NOTES: n=38. Response options were: (1) Disagree, (2), Agree, and (3), Don't know. The first and fourth statements are factually correct, while the second and their statements are incorrect.

[a] Due to item nonresponse, n=36 PVAAS district administrators for this item.

Table 4.14
Pilot District Administrators' Reporting of the Availability and Usefulness of PVAAS Resources

PVAAS Resource	Percentage of Pilot District Administrators (n=37) Who Reported Having Access to This Resource	Of Those Who Had Access to the Resource, the Percentage Who Reported Finding It Moderately or Very Useful
The *Introductory Guide for Pennsylvania Educators* ("Understanding Value-Added Analysis")	95	68
The *Resource Guide for the Pennsylvania Value-Added Assessment System* prepared by SAS	95	73
The "PVAAS Overview" presentation	93	81
Workshops on PVAAS provided by the district, intermediate unit, or state	95	79
Other information on PVAAS provided on district or PDE Internet sites (*not* the site where PVAAS scores are reported; i.e., https://pvaas.sas.com)	86	57
Other articles, books, or Internet sites related to value-added assessment	85	58

NOTES: Response options were (1) I have not seen or participated in this, (2) Not useful, (3) Minimally useful, (4) Moderately useful, and (5) Very useful. The denominator used to calculate the percentage reporting moderately or very useful was the number of administrators who reported that they had seen or participated in the resource, that is, who responded with options 2 through 5.

vides. About 95 percent of the administrators have seen the *Introductory Guide for Pennsylvania Educators ("Understanding Value-Added Analysis")* and among those familiar with the guide, slightly more that two-thirds found it moderately to very useful. Similarly large percentages of administrators have seen the *Resource Guide for the Pennsylvania Value-Added Assessment System* and the "PVAAS Overview" presentation and found them useful and attended state-supported workshops on PVAAS and found them useful. Administrators were less likely to have seen additional documents on the PDE website or from other sources, and among those administrators who accessed these alternative sources, only a little more than half reported that they were useful.

Summary

Overall, there are few differences between the survey responses of the PVAAS and the comparison administrators. As was expected, PVAAS administrators indicated greater access to growth data and greater use of such data. PVAAS administrators reported greater investment in resources for data analysis for their staffs than their counterparts in the comparison districts, and they appear to be somewhat more knowledgeable about growth data, although differences on individual items are small and not statistically significant.

Administrators in pilot districts clearly value the PVAAS program and reported a number of ways in which they believe it has affected practice and attitudes in their districts. There appear to be a number of barriers to effective use, however, and it is not clear that PVAAS is driving many of the decisions superintendents make. Use of PVAAS is substantially less extensive than use of achievement data more generally.

CHAPTER FIVE

Principals' Responses to PVAAS

This chapter presents results from the principal surveys. One of the goals of the principal surveys was to examine how participating in PVAAS affects principals' attitudes and opinions about standardized test-score data and use of that data. The second goal was to understand how principals use the PVAAS data. However, one of the key findings from our surveys of principals from schools in PVAAS districts is that although nearly all of them reported having heard of PVAAS, large numbers of these principals reported that they had not seen the PVAAS reports, and a small percentage also incorrectly reported that their school is not participating in PVAAS. Table 5.1 provides the distribution of the sample, both unweighted and weighted, broken down by the principal's level of engagement with PVAAS, where the criteria for being considered engaged in PVAAS are having seen the school's PVAAS reports and having knowledge of the school's status with the pilot program.

Principals with very little engagement with PVAAS are unlikely to be affected by the program, and comparisons of unengaged principals from PVAAS districts to other principals are unlikely to provide meaningful information about the effects of experience with a value-added system. Hence we restricted our comparisons of non-PVAAS and PVAAS principals to include only the 60 responding PVAAS principals who reported they were engaged in PVAAS, by reporting knowledge of the school's status with the pilot program and having seen the PVAAS reports for their school. For these comparisons, we weighted the responses from the comparison group principals so that the school and district characteristics from the two groups were similar, using the methods described in Chapter Two. The results of these comparisons are presented below.

We also studied the characteristics of principals who report engagement in PVAAS compared to those who do not. As shown in Table 5.2, engaged principals were more likely to be

Table 5.1
Familiarity with PVAAS of Principals from PVAAS Districts

Level of Familiarity	Sample Count	Weighted Count	Estimated Distribution
Reported that school is not participating in PVAAS or status is unknown	24	69	28.3%
Reported that school is participating in PVAAS but did not see report	19	34	14.0%
Reported seeing PVAAS report	60	141	57.7%

NOTES: Twenty-one survey respondents failed to complete these items. Weighted for sampling and nonresponse.

Table 5.2
School and Principal Characteristics for Principals Who Were or Were Not Engaged in PVAAS

Variable	Not Engaged (n=43)	Engaged (n=60)
Cohort 1	**0.91**	**0.62**
Community type		
Urban	0.49	0.30
Suburban	0.22	0.21
Rural	0.29	0.49
Percentage of Hispanic students	**18.11**	**11.44**
Percentage of African-American student	**21.88**	**9.07**
Percentage of white students	**57.88**	**77.58**
Percentage of low-income students	41.77	35.61
Average scaled mathematic score[a]	−0.02	0.28
Average scaled reading score[a]	−0.09	0.17
Principal new to school[b]	**0.40**	**0.09**

NOTES: Variables that are significant ($p < 0.05$) predictors of engagement are in boldface type. Values are weighted by nonresponse and sampling weights.

[a] 2002 PSSA scores scaled so to have a mean of zero and standard deviation one by grade.

[b] Principal tenure at school is less than two years.

from rural schools and from schools serving larger percentages of white students and smaller percentages of African-American, Hispanic, or low-income students. They were less likely to be within their first two years at their current school, and their students tended to score above average on the PSSA mathematics and reading tests. Cohort 2 principals were more likely than Cohort 1 principals to be engaged in PVAAS. In multivariate models, principal tenure, cohort, and percentage of African-American students were significantly related to engagement. Even after controlling for other factors, the odds of being engaged were only 11 percent as large for principals who were new to their schools as for other principals. A 10-percentage-point increase in the percentage of black students corresponds to about a 30 percent reduction in the odds of a principal being engaged. Even controlling for other factors, the odds of being engaged were about 20 percent as large for principals from Cohort 1 than those from Cohort 2.

Another potential influence on principal engagement with PVAAS is the district's involvement in PVAAS. To measure district involvement with PVAAS we created a scale of PVAAS use from the items in Table 4.10. Exploratory factor analysis suggested that the items formed one primary factor, but some items were weakly correlated with that factor. Hence our PVAAS use scale equals the number items for which the district administrator reported moderate to extensive use among the following:

- make changes to the district's curriculum and instructional materials
- monitor schools' implementation of curricula or use of resources
- focus principal and/or teacher professional development

- evaluate the effectiveness of specific programs
- communicate with parents or other community members.

Scores ranged from 0 to 5 with an average of 1.6 and standard deviation of 1.7; 42 percent of the 38 responding district administrators scored 0, 18 percent scored 1, 5 percent scored 2, 8 percent scored 3, 21 percent scored 4, and 5 percent scored 5.

The districts PVAAS-use scale score was positively associated with engagement, although with our small sample size, the relationship was not statistically significant. If we controlled for cohort and percent of black students in the school, p-value for the PVAAS-use scale score in a logistic regression for predicting engagement was 0.06. Using one additional item is associated with a 32 percent increase in the odds that principal is engaged. However, principals at all levels of district PVAAS reported being engaged in the program. For example, 50 percent of the principals in districts with zero use reported being engaged in the program. Similarly, district use does not guarantee principal engagement; over a quarter of principals from districts with use scores of 4 or 5 reported not being engaged.

The remainder of this chapter begins with a comparison of engaged PVAAS principals to principals from similar schools in the non-PVAAS districts on their responses to items about data use and attitudes about data and testing. In this comparison, we reweighted the responses from principals in the comparison districts to match the subset of engaged PVAAS principals in terms of the distribution of school and district characteristics. In general, the survey items parallel the items from the superintendent surveys to facilitate comparisons of the responses from these two groups of educators.

Actions and Opinions in PVAAS and Comparison Districts

We compared the two groups on several sets of questions addressing use of achievement data, opinions about test-based accountability, and perceived facilitators and barriers to effective data use. Each set of results is presented below.

Use of Achievement Data

A goal of VAA systems such as PVAAS is to engage educators in using growth data to support decisionmaking, in addition to status measures such as the percent of students scoring proficient on the state test. We conjectured that participation in PVAAS might change principals' perceptions of the utility of various data sources.

As shown in Table 5.3, our survey results provide little evidence that the exposure to growth data through PVAAS changes principals' attitudes about data sources. Although the engaged principals from the PVAAS districts were significantly more likely than principals in the comparison districts to report that data on student growth is very useful (52 percent versus 38 percent), they were not less likely than comparison principals to view status measures as very useful. In fact, they tended to be more likely to view status measures as very useful, although these differences tend to be small and none are statistically significant.

A large percentage of principals from both groups (73 percent of engaged principals from the pilot districts and 66 percent of principals from the comparison districts) reported that the percentage of students at each performance level on the state's accountability test, the PSSA, is very useful for informing their efforts to improve students' performance. The percentages of

Table 5.3
Principals' Views on the Usefulness of Various Sources of Information for Improving Student Performance

Source of Information	Percentage of Principals Who Reported That the Source Is Very Useful	
	Engaged PVAAS Pilot Principals (n=60)	Comparison Principals (n=115)
Percentage of students at each performance level (basic, proficient, etc.) on either the Pennsylvania System of School Assessment (PSSA) or district standardized tests	73	66
Scale scores (e.g., percentile ranks, NCEs, grade equivalent scores) on PSSA or district standardized tests_	47	44
Schoolwide results on the PSSA or district standardized tests summarized for each student subgroup (e.g., special education, race/ethnicity, economically disadvantaged)[a]	57	56
Schoolwide results on the PSSA or district standardized tests broken down by topic or skill[a]	66	63
Student performance on interim or diagnostic assessments (e.g., DIBELS, DRA, or district-developed interim assessments)	66	60
Reports of individual student *growth* in achievement from one year to the next on any achievement test	**52**	**38**
Analysis or reports provided by a school-based data team (i.e., a team of teachers and/or administrators tasked with analyzing and summarizing student achievement test results)[b]	68	49

NOTES: Statistically significant differences are indicated by bold typeface (p < 0.05). Response options were (1) Not available or haven't heard of this, (2) Not useful, (3) Minimally useful (4) Moderately useful, and (5) Very useful.

[a] Due to item nonresponse, n=114 comparison principals for this item.

[b] Due to item nonresponse, n=59 PVAAS principals for this item.

principals in both groups who reported that the performance level information is very useful (73 percent of the PVAAS principals and 66 percent of comparison principals) were greater than the percentages who reported that other summaries of students' level of performance, such as scale scores or normal curve equivalents, are very useful (47 percent of the PVAAS principals and 44 percent of comparison principals). Most importantly, the proportion of principals in the PVAAS group who reported that performance level data are very useful was greater than the proportion who reported that growth data are very useful (73 percent versus 52 percent). Moreover, on an additional survey question in which principals reported the three data sources from the list in Table 5.3 that are most useful for improving student performance, only 25 percent of the engaged PVAAS principals reported that growth data was one of these. This compares with 20 percent of the comparison principals. Principals' opinions about the relative utility of these different types of student achievement data are probably driven in large part by the emphasis on performance levels in state and federal accountability policies.

Engaged PVAAS principals tend to value growth data less than the PVAAS superintendents. Whereas 61 percent of district administrators reported that growth data are very useful, only 52 percent of principals gave growth data such value. This difference is consistent with less access and familiarity with the PVAAS data and less training about growth measures among principals than superintendents.

Another noteworthy (although because of the small sample, not significantly significant) difference between principals engaged in the PVAAS and comparison principals is their perception of the utility of reports from school-based data teams. The PVAAS principals were more likely than their counterparts in the comparison group to respond that such reports are very useful (68 percent versus 49 percent), and the difference results mostly from principals in comparison districts reporting that such reports are unavailable. Similar differences are found between pilot and comparison group superintendents. These differences suggest that PVAAS districts and schools are more likely than their non-PVAAS counterparts to form school data teams, though it is impossible to determine whether this difference preceded the PVAAS implementation or whether it is influenced by it.

The results also indicate strong support in both groups for results from interim assessments: About two-thirds of principals in both groups found these very useful. This type of testing has been adopted recently in large numbers of school districts (Hamilton et al., 2007) and our data suggest that it is being received enthusiastically by principals.

One important measure of the success of a VAA system is changes in data use by educators. Under the general theory of action for such systems, implementation of the system would result in changes in how principals use data for a variety of school improvement activities. Hence, we queried principals about their use of data to support a range of activities and on the frequency with which they discuss and use test scores in various settings.

Table 5.4 presents the percentage of principals reporting various uses of state and district achievement test data. Even though this analysis focused on PVAAS principals who were at least minimally engaged, PVAAS does not appear to affect principals' uses of test scores for the practices we investigated. There are no significant differences between the groups. In general, the vast majority of principals reported using test scores for most tasks. The most common usage was identifying low-performing students, followed by identifying and correcting gaps in the curriculum and instruction of students. Principals in the pilot districts were also more likely to report moderate to extensive use of test scores for identifying high-performing students for additional enrichment (75 percent versus 60 percent), assigning students or teachers to instructional groups (68 percent versus 55 percent), and evaluating the effectiveness of specific programs (63 percent versus 55 percent), although none of these differences are statistically significant.

Support for Test-Based Accountability

As noted in our discussion of district administrator responses in Chapter Four, the provision of PVAAS information could change the level of enthusiasm for testing and accountability, conceivably in either direction. Again, the data do not provide evidence of any PVAAS effects. There are no statistically significant differences and just two notable differences between the engaged pilot principals and similar principals from the comparison group on their attitudes and opinions about the accountability systems and NCLB. Principals in the pilot districts were considerably more likely to report that the NCLB accountability system has been beneficial for their schools (65 percent versus 53 percent), and they were also more likely to report that, because of pressure to meet the AYP target, they and their staffs are focusing more on improving student achievement than would have been otherwise (77 percent versus 64 percent). These differences indicate greater support among the PVAAS principals for the traditional accountability systems based on levels of student achievement rather than growth. Our expectations

Table 5.4
Principals' Use of State and District Achievement Test Results for Various Purposes in 2004–2005 and 2005–2006

Purpose	Percentage of Principals Who Reported Moderate or Extensive Use of Achievement Test Results for This Purpose	
	Engaged PVAAS Pilot Principals (n=60)	Comparison Principals (n=114)
Develop a school improvement plan	78	78
Identify low-performing students who need additional assistance[a]	98	96
Identify high-performing students who need additional enrichment[a]	75	60
Identify and correct gaps in the curriculum and instruction for all students	88	83
Communicate with parents	70	66
Set different learning goals for different students or classes	68	67
Assign or reassign students to teachers or instructional groups	68	55
Focus teacher professional development[b]	78	80
Identify teacher strengths and weaknesses[b]	42	43
Evaluate the effectiveness of specific programs	63	55
Celebrate staff or student accomplishments[c]	73	78

NOTES: None of the differences between engaged PVAAS principals and comparison principals is statistically significant (p < 0.05). Response options were (1) Did not use in the way, (2) Used minimally, (3) Used moderately, and (4) Used extensively.

[a] Due to item nonresponse, n=59 PVAAS principals for this item.

[b] Due to item nonresponse, n=113 comparison principals for this item.

[c] Due to item nonresponse, n=112 comparison principals for this item.

were that exposure to PVAAS and its training would make educators less supportive of levels-based accountability.

Data from another set of survey items not shown in the tables indicate that principals from the two groups also report similar attitudes among their staffs toward data use. About 82 percent of PVAAS-engaged principals reported that teachers in their schools share in a belief in the value of data for school improvement, compared to 75 percent of the principals in the comparison group. Similarly, there is almost no difference in the percentage of principals reporting that teachers in their school use assessment data for instructional planning or to improve their instruction (78 percent versus 73 percent).

Facilitators and Barriers

A key factor that is likely to influence how VAA changes principals' use of data is the support that they receive for using data. Hence, it is important to understand how facilitators of data use, such as training for the principals and their staffs, differ between the engaged principals and the comparison group. Conversely, participation in VAA might also change principals' perceptions of barriers they face to effective use of data for school improvement. The next few

Table 5.5
Principals' Opinions About the State's Accountability System Under NCLB, Including PSSA Testing and Designation of AYP Status

Statement	Percentage of Principals Who Agreed or Strongly Agreed	
	Engaged PVAAS Pilot Principals (n=60)	Comparison Principals (n=113)
Overall, the state's NCLB accountability system has been beneficial for students at my school.[a]	65	53
The state's NCLB accountability system leaves little time to teach content not on the PSSA.	70	67
As a result of the state's NCLB accountability system, high-achieving students are not receiving appropriately challenging curriculum or instruction.[b]	35	42
We have made substantial changes in the school's curriculum and instructional strategies to improve student performance on the PSSA.[b]	83	77
PSSA scores accurately reflect the achievement of students in my school.[c]	45	43
My school's AYP status accurately reflects the overall performance of our school.[c]	55	54
Differences in student characteristics from year to year make it difficult for my school to make AYP.[c]	47	54
Because of pressure to meet the AYP target, my staff and I are focusing more on improving student achievement than we would without the AYP target.[a]	77	64
The state's NCLB accountability system does not adequately consider student growth.[d]	83	81

NOTES: None of the differences between engaged PVAAS principals and comparison principals is statistically significant (p < 0.05). Response options were (1) Strongly disagree, (2) Disagree, (3) Agree, and (4) Strongly agree.

[a] Due to item nonresponse, n=111 comparison principals for this item.

[b] Due to item nonresponse, n=112 comparison principals for this item.

[c] Due to item nonresponse, n=110 comparison principals for this item.

[d] Due to item nonresponse, n=58 PVAAS and n=112 comparison principals for this item.

tables explore these issues. Tables 5.6 and 5.7 focus on resources and training provided to the principals to support data use and accountability, and Tables 5.8 and 5.9 focus on the support the principals provided or wanted for their teachers. Table 5.10 provides information about barriers to data use.

The engaged pilot principals were more likely than comparison principals to receive training on how to use test-score data for instructional planning (90 percent versus 73 percent, p < 0.05). Engaged pilot principals were also much more likely than the comparison principals to receive information on data system or guidance on selecting these systems (81 percent versus 68 percent, p=0.06). These activities could easily reflect the effects of PVAAS participation, given the nature of the PVAAS training. Outside of these differences, the groups were similar in the resources they received, but somewhat greater percentages of the engaged PVAAS principals tended to view the resources favorably.

Table 5.6
Principals' Reporting on the Availability and Usefulness of Various PVAAS Resources

Resource	Percentage of Principals Who Reported That the Resource Was Available		Of Those Who Reported That the Resource Was Available, the Percentage Who Reported That It Was Moderately or Very Useful	
	Engaged PVAAS Pilot Principals (n=59)	Comparison Principals (n=114)	Engaged PVAAS Pilot Principals	Comparison Principals
Workshops or meetings where test results are presented and explained[a]	85	82	88	79
Training on how to use test results for instructional planning or school improvement[a]	**90**	**73**	91	83
Information on available data analysis systems and/or guidance on selecting these systems[b]	81	68	73	61
Technical assistance with data analysis[a]	76	77	73	68
Technical assistance with technology	80	86	72	69

NOTES: Statistically significant differences are indicated by bold typeface ($p < 0.05$). Response options were (1) Not available, (2) Available and not useful, (3) Available and minimally useful, (4) Available and moderately useful, and (5) Available and very useful. The denominators for columns 3 and 4 were the numbers of principals who reported that the resource was available, that is, who responded with options 2 through 5.

[a] Due to item nonresponse, n=113 comparison principals for this item.

[b] Due to item nonresponse, n=111 comparison principals for this item.

Table 5.7 shows no sizable differences between engaged pilot principals and comparison group principals in their reports on their professional development activities. A large majority of principals in both groups reported attending professional development with an emphasis on analyzing student achievement, using assessment results to guide school improvement, helping teachers to understand standards and curriculum materials, and meeting the needs of low-achieving students. Most of these activities were slightly more common in the comparison group.

For both groups, professional development with a focus on analyzing student achievement data was most prevalent (81 percent for the pilot group and 88 percent for the comparison group), and the difference between groups is significant. This is a somewhat surprising result, because PVAAS is a tool for using assessment results to guide school improvement, and we would have hypothesized that pilot district principals would be more likely to receive professional development in this area as part of their PVAAS training. It may be that PVAAS training displaced other training the principals would have received on this topic. It is also possible that, with the impending state rollout of PVAAS and the current popularity of data-driven decisionmaking, this sort of professional development is more available for all principals but that the comparison group principals were more likely to attend because they had not previously received the PVAAS training.

Participation in the PVAAS pilot program had no effect on the emphasis placed on teacher training for these school districts, according to the principals' reports (Table 5.8). Nearly all principals in both groups reported that aligning curriculum and instruction with

Table 5.7
The Emphasis on Various Topic Areas in Principals' Personal Professional Development Activities During the Prior (2004–2005) and Current (2005–2006) School Years

Topic Area	Percentage of Principals Who Reported That the Topic Was a Moderate or Major Emphasis	
	Engaged PVAAS Pilot Principals (n=58)	Comparison Principals (n=108)
Managing staff or resources[a]	38	36
Understanding the requirements of the accountability system under NCLB[b]	67	70
Analyzing student achievement data	81	88
Using assessment results to guide school improvement[a]	79	83
Working to engage parents in support of the school's efforts[a]	34	32
Helping teachers understand standards and use curriculum materials	72	70
Meeting the needs of low-achieving students	78	84

NOTES: The term "school year" includes the summer. Statistically significant differences are indicated by bold typeface ($p < 0.05$). Response options were (1) No emphasis, (2) Minor emphasis, (3) Moderate emphasis, and (4) Major emphasis.

[a] Due to item nonresponse, n=107 comparison principals for this item.

[b] Due to item nonresponse, n=106 comparison principals for this item.

Table 5.8
Teachers' Professional Development Priorities for the 2005–2006 School Year, as Reported by Principals

Area of Professional Development	Percentage of Principals Who Reported That the Area Was a Medium or High Priority for Teachers at Their Schools	
	Engaged PVAAS Pilot Principals (n=60)	Comparison Principals (n=113)
Aligning curriculum and instruction with the Pennsylvania Academic Standards	92	89
Aligning curriculum and instruction with the Pennsylvania Assessment Anchors[a]	92	94
Analyzing and interpreting student achievement data[a]	92	91
Using achievement data to guide instruction	95	93
Familiarizing students with state or district test format and test-taking strategies	92	90
Reviewing and implementing a school improvement plan	77	66

NOTES: The term "school year" includes the summer. None of the differences between engaged PVAAS principals and comparison principals is statistically significant ($p < 0.05$). Response options were (1) Not a priority, (2) Low priority, (3) Medium priority, (4) High priority.

[a] Due to item nonresponse, n=112 comparison principals for this item.

Table 5.9
Principals' Efforts to Help Teachers Prepare Students for the PSSA

Activity	Percentage of Principals Who Reported Engaging in the Activity	
	Engaged PVAAS Pilot Principals (n=60)	Comparison Principals (n=114)
Distributed commercial test-preparation materials (e.g., practice tests)	**97**	**77**
Distributed released copies of the PSSA tests or items	92	96
Discussed methods for preparing students for the PSSA at staff meetings	97	95
Encouraged or required teachers to spend more time on tested subjects and less time on other subjects	67	58
Helped teachers identify content that is likely to appear on the PSSA so they can cover it adequately in their instruction	97	99
Encouraged teachers to focus on students *close* to meeting standards (e.g., close to proficient)	82	76
Discussed the state's Assessment Anchors with teachers[a]	100	99
Encouraged or required teachers to create ability-based student groups to prepare for PSSA[a]	57	38

NOTES: Statistically significant differences are indicated by bold typeface (p < 0.05). Response options were (1) No and (2) Yes.

[a] Due to item nonresponse, n=113 comparison principals for this item.

the state standards and the Assessment Anchors was of medium or high priority. Similarly, nearly all principals reported that training on analyzing and interpreting student achievement data and using data to guide instruction was of medium or high importance for teachers in their schools. The vast majority of principals in both groups also reported that teacher professional development on familiarizing students with test formats and test-taking strategies was of high or medium importance for teachers in their schools. For both groups, professional development for teachers focused on school improvement plans was least likely to be of medium or high importance. Principals engaged in PVAAS were more likely than their counterparts in control districts to report that this type of training was a priority for their teachers (77 percent versus 66 percent), but the difference is not statistically significant.

Again, it would be reasonable to hypothesize that participation in PVAAS would increase emphasis on training teachers to use test-score data to improve instruction. However, given the extreme emphasis on improving test scores in all schools, it appears that there is little room for PVAAS alone to increase attention on using test scores to drive instruction.

As was found with the district administrators, majorities of principals in both groups participated in activities focused directly on improving test scores. In general, principals from the pilot districts appear to be somewhat more aggressive at directing energy toward improving test scores. The PVAAS-engaged principals were more likely to report distributing commercial test-preparation materials (97 percent versus 77 percent, p < 0.01). They were also slightly to modestly (but not significantly) more likely to report discussing methods for preparing students for the state test (97 percent versus 95 percent), encouraging teachers to spend more time on tested subjects (67 percent versus 58 percent), encouraging teachers to focus on students close to meeting standards (82 percent versus 76 percent), and encouraging or requiring teachers to create ability-based student groups to prepare for PSSA (57 percent versus 38 percent). It is not clear why PVAAS participation would result in the specific differences we find between the groups. Activities such as use of commercial test-preparation materials or focusing on tested subjects or students close to but not proficient are not related to growth data or encouraged in the PVAAS training materials. It is possible that these are collateral events resulting from a greater focus on testing or some other unforeseen aspect of participation. It is also possible that they indicate differences between the groups that are unrelated to PVAAS participation. We discuss these issues more fully in Chapter Seven.

Table 5.10 shows that, although few principals in both groups reported that any of the factors other than timing of the test data hinders their ability to use test scores, principals engaged with PVAAS were less likely than principals from similar schools in the comparison group to report that various factors are hindrances to effective use of achievement data to improve outcomes. Generally, the differences are not significant. However, the difference between groups is quite large for the factor "lack of information on student achievement growth." Over half of the comparison group principals (57 percent) reported that lack of data on student growth is a hindrance, but only 27 percent of the engaged pilot principals reported that this as a hindrance. Clearly, this difference must be due in part to the information provided by PVAAS. This difference parallels the finding for district administrators.

Understanding and Interpretation of Growth Data

Much of the PVAAS training has focused on the interpretation of growth and the value of growth data for decisionmaking. Hence, we hypothesized that engaged principals in pilot districts would have different opinions and understanding about growth in student achievement than their counterparts in the comparison districts. This does not appear to be the case. As shown in Table 5.11, there are no significant differences between principals on questions about interpreting student achievement growth. However, many fewer PVAAS-engaged principals than comparison group principals agreed or strongly agreed with inaccurate statements that growth is strongly related to student attributes (i.e., 36 percent versus 52 percent for the statement "the growth that students attain each year is strongly related to their overall intelligence," and 27 percent versus 37 percent for the statement "the poverty level or family circumstances of students are more important than teacher effectiveness for determining student growth"). In contrast, about 60 percent of principals in both groups incorrectly reported that school-level changes in PSSA scores are good indicators of whether students have achieved growth.

Responses to PVAAS Among Principals from Participating Districts

As discussed in Chapter Four, the PVAAS data must be accepted and used by educators for it to have an effect on student outcomes. This section discusses the responses to PVAAS of principals in the pilot program.

As noted in Table 5.1, only about 58 percent of the principals in the PVAAS districts reported seeing their PVAAS reports and knowing that their school is participating in PVAAS. It is unlikely that principals who have not seen the reports or do not know that their school is participating will be using the data constructively. Therefore, we primarily focus on the engaged principals' responses, weighted to account for differential nonresponse.

Table 5.10
Principals' Views on Whether Various Factors Hinder the Effective Use of State and District Achievement Data

Factor Affecting Data Use	Percentage of Principals Who Reported That the Factor Moderately or Greatly Hinders Effective Use of Data	
	Engaged PVAAS Pilot Principals (n=60)	Comparison Principals (n=114)
Lack of access to achievement results for students currently enrolled in this school	18	29
Difficult-to-understand reports or displays of achievement results	23	28
Insufficient technology (e.g., computers, software, high-speed Internet connection)[a]	12	14
Lack of district staff to assist me with interpretation of data[b]	18	28
Lack of school or district staff to address technology problems[c]	13	22
Lack of training for me on the interpretation and use of achievement results[d]	14	23
Teachers' lack of skills or experience with analyzing data	50	54
Lack of flexibility to alter the curriculum (e.g., because of district requirements) when test-score data reveal problems or gaps	18	24
Receiving test results late in the year[c]	83	89
Insufficient time to examine and interpret results carefully[c]	65	73
Lack of access to information about student growth in achievement[e]	**27**	**57**

NOTES: Statistically significant differences are indicated by bold typeface ($p < 0.05$). Response options were (1) Not a hindrance, (2) Slight hindrance, (3) Moderate hindrance, and (4) Great hindrance.

[a] Due to item nonresponse, n=59 PVAAS and n=113 comparison principals for this item.

[b] Due to item nonresponse, n=110 comparison principals for this item.

[c] Due to item nonresponse, n=112 comparison principals for this item.

[d] Due to item nonresponse, n=59 PVAAS and n=112 comparison principals for this item.

[e] Due to item nonresponse, n=113 comparison principals for this item.

Among the engaged principals who reported any familiarity with PVAAS, a large majority reported having seen each of the PVAAS introductory or training publications and taken part in training workshops. Moreover, most principals reported that the materials are moderately to very useful. In contrast, principals who were not engaged had very little exposure to the training. It is not clear if the training leads to the engagement by principals or if engaged principals seek out training, either on their own or as a result of district encouragement. However, it is clear that principals who are using PVAAS are for the most part receiving training and are finding that training useful.

Engaged principals' attitudes about PVAAS and their experiences with it varied across items, as shown in Table 5.13. Nearly 80 percent reported that PVAAS provides an accurate indication of how well their schools are improving student achievement. A majority (60

Table 5.11
Principals' Views About Student Achievement Growth on State and District Standardized Tests

Statement	Percentage of Principals Who Agreed or Strongly Agreed	
	Engaged PVAAS Pilot Principals (n=59)	Comparison Principals (n=113)
The growth that students attain each year is strongly related to their overall intelligence.	36	52
The poverty level or family circumstances of students are more important than teacher effectiveness for determining student growth.[a]	27	37
Educators have a significant influence on the progress students make in their achievement each year.	100	97
A year of exposure to an ineffective teacher can affect students' performance in future school years.	93	90
School-level changes in PSSA scores are good indicators of whether *students* in those schools have achieved growth.	63	60
A school cannot meet its performance expectations under NCLB if its students' scores are declining over time.[b]	81	82

NOTES: None of the differences between pilot and comparison districts is statistically significant ($p < 0.05$). Response options were (1) Strongly disagree, (2) Disagree, (3) Agree, and (4) Strongly agree. The third and fourth statements are generally considered factually accurate, while the remaining statements would generally be considered inaccurate.

[a] Due to item nonresponse, n=110 comparison principals for this item.

[b] Due to item nonresponse, n=11 comparison principals for this item.

percent) reported making changes to their leadership or school improvement efforts based on PVAAS. Similarly, 56 percent reported that PVAAS helps motivate them. However, only small percentages agreed or strongly agreed that PVAAS is discussed frequently at staff planning meetings (33 percent), has caused the school to focus more on low-performing or high-performing students (43 percent and 33 percent, respectively), is used to identify students at risk of not meeting the standards (42 percent), or helps with communications with parents (27 percent).

Principals were generally confident in their understanding of PVAAS. Only 38 percent reported uncertainty about how to interpret their school's PVAAS effects, though only half were confident they could explain conceptually how a school's mean predicted score is calculated.

Many of the items in Table 5.13 have parallels to items asked of the district administrators (Table 4.9), and for the most part principals were less likely than the district administrators to agree or strongly agree with the statements. For instance, only 27 percent of principals reported that PVAAS helps them communicate more effectively with parents about their children's progress, compared with 81 percent of district administrators. Other differences between these groups include the frequency with which PVAAS is discussed with staff (33 percent of principals and 51 percent of administrators) and the effect of PVAAS on districts' or schools' focus on low-performing students (43 percent of principals and 66 percent of administrators). Similarly, just 56 percent of engaged principals agreed with the statement that PVAAS helps to motivate them, whereas 80 percent of district administrators agreed or strongly agreed that the

Table 5.12
PVAAS-Engaged Principals' Reporting of the Availability and Usefulness of PVAAS Resources

Resource	Percentage of Engaged Principals (n=60) Who Reported Having Access to This Resource	Of Those Who Had Access to the Resource, the Percentage Who Reported Finding It Moderately or Very Useful
The *Introductory Guide for Pennsylvania Educators* ("Understanding Value-Added Analysis")	88	74
The *Resource Guide for the Pennsylvania Value-Added Assessment System* prepared by SAS	88	72
The "PVAAS Overview" presentation	88	69
Workshops on PVAAS provided by the district, intermediate unit, or state	87	74
Other information on PVAAS provided on district or PDE Internet sites (*not* the site where PVAAS scores are reported; i.e., http://evaas.sas.com)	74	69
Other articles, books, or Internet sites related to value-added assessment[a]	70	58

NOTES: Response options were (1) I have not seen or participated in this, (2) Not useful, (3) Minimally useful, (4) Moderately useful, and (5) Very useful. The denominator used to calculate the percentage reporting moderately or very useful is the number of principals who reported exposure to the resource, that is, who responded with options 2 through 5.

[a] Due to item nonresponse, n=59 for this item.

Table 5.13
PVAAS-Engaged Principals' Opinions About PVAAS

Statement	Percentage of Engaged Principals (n=59) Who Agreed or Strongly Agreed
PVAAS provides an accurate indication of how well our school is improving student achievement.	78
I have made changes to my instructional leadership or school improvement efforts in response to information from PVAAS.	60
PVAAS is discussed frequently during staff planning meetings in this school.	33
PVAAS helps me communicate more effectively with parents about their children's progress than I could without PVAAS.	27
Staff in this school use the PVAAS *projections* to identify students who are at risk of not meeting standards.	42
PVAAS has caused the school to increase its focus on low-performing students.	43
I am not sure I understand how to interpret my school's PVAAS school effect.	38
The information on student growth in PVAAS helps to motivate me because I can see my efforts paying off.	56
I am confident in my ability to explain conceptually (not necessarily mathematically) how a school's mean predicted score is calculated.	51
The school focuses more on the needs of high-achieving students because of PVAAS than we would without the information from PVAAS.[a]	33

NOTE: Response options were (1) Strongly disagree, (2) Disagree, (3) Agree, (4) Strongly agree, and (9) I don't know (9).

[a] Due to item nonresponse, n=58 for this item.

Table 5.14
PVAAS-Engaged Principals' Use of PVAAS Versus State or District Achievement Test Results for Various Purposes

Purpose	Percentage of Engaged Principals Who Reported Moderate or Extensive Use of PVAAS Data for This Purpose	Percentage of Engaged Principals Who Reported Moderate or Extensive Use of State or District Achievement Test Results for This Purpose
Develop a school improvement plan	34	74
Identify low-performing students who need additional assistance	45	99
Identify high-performing students who need additional enrichment	42	80
Identify and correct gaps in the curriculum and instruction for all students	45	93
Communicate with parents	10	72
Set different learning goals for different students or classes	29	96
Assign or reassign students to teachers or instructional groups	18	67
Focus teacher professional development	36	80
Identify teacher strengths and weaknesses	25	47
Evaluate the effectiveness of specific programs	35	64
Celebrate staff or student accomplishments	27	76

NOTES: n=58. Response options were (1) Did not use in this way, (2) Used minimally, (3; Used moderately, and (4) Used extensively.

information on student growth in PVAAS helps school staff because they can see their efforts paying off.

District administrators and principals were in much greater agreement about the effects of PVAAS on higher-achieving students. One third of principals agreed or strongly agreed that their school focuses more on the needs of high-achieving students because of PVAAS, and the same fraction of district administrators agreed or strongly agreed with a similar statement. Perhaps due to their more limited exposure to the PVAAS materials, principals were more likely than district administrators to agree or strongly agree with the statement "I am not sure I understand how to interpret my school's PVAAS school effect" and less likely to agree or strongly agree with the statement "I am confident in my ability to explain conceptually (not necessarily mathematically) how a school's mean predicted score is calculated."

As with the district administrators, only a minority of the engaged principals reported using PVAAS moderately or extensively to support various activities (Table 5.14). Moreover, like district administrators, principals were roughly two or more times more likely to report using other state or district test results for each activity. Identifying teacher strengths and weaknesses is the least common usage of both PVAAS and state or district test results. The most common usage of PVAAS was for identifying low-performing students, followed by identifying gaps in the curriculum and instruction for all students, identifying high-performing students, focusing teacher professional development, and developing school improvement plans. These are also the tasks for which very large proportions of principals reported using other test results.

Table 5.15
PVAAS-Engaged Principals' Reporting of Whether They Saw Various PVAAS Report Components and Whether They Found Them Useful

PVAAS Report Component	Percentage of Principals (n=58) Who Reported Seeing the Component	Of Those Who Saw the Component, the Percentage Who Reported That It Was Moderately or Very Useful
School-level reports (table form)[a]	95	70
Graphs showing growth among students in different quintiles (part of the school-level diagnostic reports)	92	74
Graphs showing growth among students in the advanced, proficient, etc., categories (part of the school-level diagnostic reports)	89	78
Subgroup reports (results disaggregated by race/ethnicity, socioeconomic status, etc.)	83	74
Student-level reports of past performance	87	69
Student-level projections of future performance	86	73
Other custom reports prepared by your school or district staff	47	54
Summary reports for individual teachers[a]	53	82
The "hints" feature on the PVAAS reporting Web site	33	70

NOTES: Response options were (1) Have not seen this, (2) I have seen it and it was Not useful, (3) I have seen it and it was Minimally useful, (4) I have seen it and it was Moderately useful, and (5) I have seen it and it was Very useful. The denominator used to calculate the percentage reporting moderately to very useful is the number of principals who reported seeing the component, that is, who responded with options 2 through 5.

[a] Due to item nonresponse, n=57 for this item.

As shown in Table 5.15, most of the engaged principals reported seeing each component of the PVAAS reports. Nearly half also reported seeing custom reports prepared by the district, and just over half reported seeing summary reports for individual teachers. PVAAS does not provide reports on individual teachers, so these reports must be created by school or district staff. Among those principals who see such teacher reports, they were considered valuable, with 82 percent reporting they are moderately to very useful. In general, most principals who see each component reported that it is moderately to very useful.

Consistent with the principals' positive ratings on the utility of the PVAAS reports, a majority agreed that the reports are clear and easy to understand. However, as shown in Table 5.16, in general the principals' opinions about PVAAS were not overly positive. For example, only 38 percent of engaged principals agreed or strongly agreed that the information from PVAAS is more useful than other PSSA data or that they refer to PVAAS frequently when planning school improvement. About the same percentage reported that PVAAS arrives early enough to be useful. Over half agreed or strongly agreed that they receive so many reports on students that it is hard to know which reports to focus on, and about a quarter agreed that their school's performance looks better with PVAAS. This general lack of enthusiasm for the information in PVAAS might explain why only a small percentage of engaged principals reported using the data to support improvement activities.

PVAAS methodology is complex, and the data (shown in Table 5.17) indicate that few principals adequately understand the meaning of the reports or the methods underlying them.

Table 5.16
PVAAS-Engaged Principals' Opinions About PVAAS Reports

Statement	Percentage of Engaged Principals (n=58) Who Agreed or Strongly Agreed
The PVAAS reports are clear and easy to understand.	67
The information I receive from PVAAS is more useful for my instructional leadership and school improvement efforts than the PSSA scores I receive from other sources.	38
I refer to the PVAAS reports frequently throughout the year when planning my school improvement efforts.	38
I receive so many different reports on student achievement that I find it hard to figure out which reports to focus on.	51
The PVAAS proficiency graphs in the school-level diagnostic report provide essentially the same information as the PSSA reports we receive from the state.[a]	27
Because PVAAS focuses on growth and the state's accountability system focuses on proficiency levels, staff in this school sometimes feel like they are forced to meet conflicting goals.	43
Our school's performance looks better when evaluated according to growth on PVAAS rather than according to AYP status.	27
The PVAAS reports are available early enough in the school year to be useful.	39

NOTE: Response options were (1) Strongly disagree, (2) Disagree, (3) Agree, (4) Strongly agree, and (9) I don't know.

[a] Due to item nonresponse, n=57 for this item.

[b] Due to item nonresponse, n=56 for this item.

We asked principals to indicate their agreement or disagreement with a set of statements about interpreting PVAAS results. The first statement addresses the meaning of the school-effect estimate provided by PVAAS—in particular, the meaning of the "no detectable difference" (NDD) designation. This designation is given when the results for a particular subject and grade do not provide statistically reliable evidence of performance that differs from the average growth over the course of a year. Only 46 percent of the engaged principals knew that, in the PVAAS reports, a school with no detectable difference is a school where the students made what PVAAS considers a year's worth of growth in achievement.[1] This is a key summary of the school's performance, and misinterpreting this label could result in a major misunderstanding of the data. In addition, only about half of the principals understood that the PVAAS measures for individual students are influenced by other students' performance, and about half mistakenly endorsed the statement that a school's grade-5 effect indicates effectiveness of earlier grades in addition to grade 5. By contrast, it is encouraging that only 23 percent of principals confused the PVAAS growth measures with school improvement or cohort-to-cohort change measures, as shown by responses to the statement about the meaning of a negative school effect for grade 5. Similarly, nearly three-quarters of the principals knew that PVAAS provides measures of student progress and not just their level of achievement.

---

[1] The PVAAS methodology changed with the 2006 reports, and facts about PVAAS presented in these items might no longer be true.

Table 5.17
PVAAS-Engaged Principals' Understanding of PVAAS School Effects and Student-Level Projections

Statement	Percentage of Engaged Principals Who Agreed or Disagreed	Percentage of Engaged Principals Who Answered "I Don't Know"
A school that is assigned a PVAAS school effect of NDD (no detectable difference) has achieved a year's worth of growth in student achievement.[a]	46	27
The PVAAS school effect for grade 5 provides an indication of school effectiveness for all tested grades up to and including grade 5.[a]	46	26
A negative PVAAS school effect for grade 5 indicates that 5th graders this year scored lower on average than 5th graders last year.	23	15
PVAAS measures of individual student growth depend not only on the student's current and previous scores but on the scores attained by other students.[a]	47	17

NOTES: n=58. Responses were (1) Disagree, (2) Agree, and (3) I don't know. Correct responses for the four statements are Agree, Disagree, Disagree, Agree. The first and fourth statements are factually correct, while the second and their statements are incorrect.

[a] Due to item nonresponse, n=57 for this item.

Summary

Principals serve a key role in translating the provision of PVAAS information into improved student achievement. As the instructional leaders of their schools, principals must understand the information provided by PVAAS and must use it effectively, along with information from other sources, to make decisions about curriculum, instruction, and professional development. The results presented in this chapter suggest a low level of engagement with PVAAS on the part of many principals, and few differences in the actions taken by principals engaged in the PVAAS pilot program and their counterparts from nonparticipating schools. Responses to questions about specific uses of PVAAS indicate that many principals are in fact using the information, but not as extensively as they use the PSSA scores provided by the state. These data also suggest that although most principals find some types of PVAAS reports to be useful, there is still widespread lack of understanding of some aspects of the PVAAS program and the measures it produces. The next chapter examines some of the same issues but with a focus on teachers.

CHAPTER SIX

Teachers' Responses to PVAAS

PVAAS is intended to facilitate effective use of achievement data for instructional decision-making. To the extent that providing PVAAS information leads to improved student achievement, it is likely that this effect occurs in large part as a result of actions taken by teachers. This chapter summarizes information from the teacher surveys. The surveys were designed to elicit information about teacher support for the PVAAS program and their understanding and use of the information that the program provides. As noted in Chapter Five, principals' survey responses suggest that in many schools the information has not yet been used by or disseminated to staff. The teacher survey results corroborate these findings. Table 6.1 summarizes information on the familiarity with the program reported by teachers in PVAAS pilot districts. Fewer than half of these teachers had even heard of PVAAS, and only 4 percent reported being very familiar with it.

We excluded from the analysis those teachers who reported that they had never heard of the program, and asked the remaining teachers whether or not their school was participating in PVAAS during the year that the survey was administered. Although all of these teachers' schools were part of PVAAS pilot districts, only 47 percent of teachers responded in the affirmative. Thirteen percent reported that their schools were not participating, and the remaining 40 percent reported that they didn't know. Combined with the results presented in Table 6.1, these numbers indicate that for the majority of teachers, PVAAS is unlikely to exert a significant direct effect on practice. As with the principals, our comparisons of PVAAS and non-PVAAS districts are restricted to those teachers who appear to be at least minimally engaged in PVAAS. The definition of "engaged" is fairly generous: An engaged teacher is one who reports having heard about PVAAS and who correctly answers that his or her school is participating in the pilot. This definition produced 108 teachers in the PVAAS sample. We weighted the

Table 6.1
Familiarity with PVAAS Among Teachers from PVAAS Districts

Level of Familiarity	Percentage of Teachers with This Level of Familiarity (weighted)
I've never heard of it.	54
I've heard of it, but don't know much about it.	23
I'm somewhat familiar with it.	19
I'm very familiar with it.	4

NOTE: Based on responses from 463 teachers in schools participating in the PVAAS pilot program. Percentages are weighted for sampling and nonresponse.

responses from the comparison group sample to create a comparison group of teachers with similar characteristics as the engaged PVAAS teachers, using the methods described in Chapter Two. Thus, the material presented next is based on a comparison of 108 engaged PVAAS teachers with a matched sample of teachers from districts not participating in PVAAS. It is important to point out that teachers explicitly identified as engaged with PVAAS may have experiences or characteristics that are associated with high levels of data use, such as prior training or a supportive school environment. Because we could not match on these unmeasured characteristics, there may be unobserved differences between the PVAAS and comparison groups that influence the results reported in this chapter. This limitation is discussed in greater detail in Chapter Seven.

We also studied the characteristics of teachers who reported engagement in PVAAS compared to those who did not. As shown in Table 6.2, teachers in rural schools with predominantly white students who tend to score above average on the PSSA test were more likely to be engaged. Teachers in urban schools with larger proportions of minority students were less likely to be engaged. Because of colinearity, none of the variables is significant in multivariate models to predict engagement. The characteristics of the schools of engaged teachers are similar to the characteristics of schools with greater principal engagement. There is less difference between cohorts in the probability of being engaged in PVAAS for teachers than there is for principals, but Cohort 2 teachers were more likely to be engaged.

Table 6.2
School Characteristics for Teachers Who Were or Were Not Engaged in PVAAS

Variable	Not Engaged (n=356)	Engaged (n=108)
Cohort 1	0.73	0.57
Community type[a]		
Urban	**0.45**	**0.22**
Suburban	**0.24**	**0.20**
Rural	**0.31**	**0.58**
Percentage of Hispanic students	15.77	6.40
Percentage of African-American students	**18.16**	**8.19**
Percentage of white students	**64.10**	**82.38**
Percentage low-income students	39.00	29.50
Average scaled mathematics score[b]	0.08	0.30
Average scaled reading score[b]	0.01	0.23

NOTE: Variables that are significant ($p < 0.05$) predictors of engagement are in boldface type. Values weighted by nonresponse and sampling weights.

[a] A joint 2 degree-of-freedom test for community type was significant in a model for predicting engagement.

[b] 2002 PSSA scores scaled so to have a mean of 0 and standard deviation 1 by grade.

As with the principals, we also found that district use of PVAAS predicted a statistically significant increase in the odds that at teacher was engaged in PVAAS. A one-item increase in the use score is associated with a 53-percentage-point increase in the odds that a teacher was engaged. District use was very important for teachers to be engaged. If the district was not using PVAAS (PVAAS use scale score of zero) the odds are only .21 that a teacher would use PVAAS. However, district use is not enough to ensure engagement. Forty-six percent of the teachers from districts with scores of 4 or 5 were not engaged.

Principal engagement is also a moderate predictor of teacher engagement. On average, at schools where the principal was PVAAS engaged, about 30 percent of teachers were also engaged; at schools where the principal was not engaged, only 17 percent of teachers were engaged; and at schools where the principal was not engaged and the district did not use PVAAS, only 7 percent of teachers were engaged. Also, district use of PVAAS appears to have a direct relationship with teacher engagement and was related to engagement even when we control for the principal's engagement.

Actions and Opinions of Teachers in PVAAS and Comparison Districts

Teachers responded to a set of questions that were similar (though not identical) to those given to principals. The questions addressed use of achievement data, opinions about test-based accountability, and perceived facilitators and barriers to effective data use. Comparisons of engaged PVAAS teachers and the matched group of non-PVAAS teachers for each of these topics are presented next.

Use of Achievement Data

Teachers reported on the availability and usefulness of a variety of types of achievement data, as shown in Table 6.3. The first set of columns indicates the percentage of teachers in each group who report that the information is available. The numbers in the second set of columns indicate the percentages of teachers who report the information is "very useful" for guiding their instruction, out of all teachers who indicated that information was available. The numbers of teachers included in the second set of columns therefore varies as a result of different levels of availability for different information sources.

The PVAAS and comparison teachers are similar in their relative rankings of both availability and usefulness of data sources. Both groups reported almost universal availability of classroom-based assessments they developed themselves, and the percentage of teachers describing this information as very useful is larger than for any other information source by a wide margin.

Only one information source is associated with a statistically significant difference between groups: the percentage of students at each performance level on the PSSA or district standardized tests. PVAAS teachers were more likely to report access to this information, and more likely to find it useful, than were their counterparts in the comparison group (97 percent versus 89 percent, $p < 0.05$). The groups appear to differ on several other items, and although the differences are not statistically significant (due in large part to the small number of teachers included in this analysis), the consistency of the direction of differences across items suggests that the PVAAS teachers generally have greater access to or awareness of most data sources and tend to find many of these more useful for instructional decisionmaking. The PVAAS teach-

Table 6.3
Teachers' Reporting of the Availability and Usefulness of Achievement Data

Type of Achievement Data	Percentage of Teachers Who Reported That the Information Was Available		Of Those Who Reported That the Resource Was Available, the Percentage of Who Reported That It Was Very Useful	
	Engaged PVAAS Pilot Teachers (n=108)	Comparison Teachers (n=528)	Engaged PVAAS Pilot Teachers	Comparison Teachers
Schoolwide results on the Pennsylvania System of School Assessment (PSSA) or district standardized tests	98	96	37	21
Percentage of students at each performance level (basic, proficient, etc.) on PSSA or district standardized tests[a]	**97**	**89**	38	25
Scale scores (e.g., percentile ranks, NCEs, grade equivalent scores) on PSSA or district standardized tests[b]	94	84	28	15
Schoolwide results on the PSSA or district standardized tests summarized for each student subgroup (e.g., special education, race/ethnicity, economically disadvantaged)[c]	90	83	21	14
Schoolwide results on the PSSA or district standardized tests broken down by topic or skill[d,e]	93	87	48	35
Student results on assessments that are provided as part of the curriculum materials (e.g., end-of-chapter tests in textbooks)[d,f]	95	93	56	50
Student results on assessments that you develop and administer in your class[g]	98	98	79	76
Student performance on interim or diagnostic assessments (e.g., DIBELS, DRA, or district-developed interim assessments)[e]	84	78	33	31
Reports of individual student *growth* in achievement from one year to the next on any achievement test[e,h]	89	72	32	27
Analysis or reports provided by a school-based data team (i.e., a team of teachers and/or administrators tasked with analyzing and summarizing student achievement test results)[c]	79	63	34	22

NOTES: Statistically significant differences are indicated by bold typeface (p < 0.05). Response options were (1) Not available or haven't heard of this, (2) Not useful, (3) Minimally useful, (4) Moderately useful, and (5) Very useful. The denominators for columns 3 and 4 were the numbers of teachers who reported that the data were available, that is, who responded with options 2 through 5.

[a] Due to item nonresponse, n=527 comparison teachers for this item.
[b] Due to item nonresponse, n=520 comparison teachers for this item.
[c] Due to item nonresponse, n=526 comparison teachers for this item.
[d] Due to item nonresponse, n=106 PVAAS teachers for this item.
[e] Due to item nonresponse, n=523 comparison teachers for this item.
[f] Due to item nonresponse, n=524 comparison teachers for this item.
[g] Due to item nonresponse, n=521 comparison teachers for this item.
[h] Due to item nonresponse, n=107 PVAAS teachers for this item.

ers tended to be more enthusiastic about state and district standardized test results in general. Among the categories of information from these tests, scores broken down by subtopic or skill were the next-most likely to be rated as very useful after performance levels. PVAAS teachers were also more likely to report having access to a school data team and to find the information provided by that team useful, and, as expected, have higher ratings of access to and usefulness of growth data.

We also asked teachers to select the three sources of information in Table 6.3 they found most useful for guiding their instruction. Both groups rated their own assessments as most useful, followed by assessments provided with curriculum materials, and PSSA or district standardized test results broken down by topic or skill. Thus, despite the importance of the PSSA for evaluating schools and providing value-added assessment results, most teachers found other sources of information more useful for instructional decisionmaking.

The next set of results examines teachers' use of state and district achievement test results during the 2004–2005 and 2004–2005 school years (Table 6.4). Reported use of test results was higher among PVAAS teachers than comparison teachers for each of the purposes included in the survey, though none of the differences are statistically significant. The most frequently endorsed item in both groups was the identification of low-performing students who need additional assistance, followed by identification and correction of gaps in curriculum and instruction for all students. Approximately half of the teachers in each group reported using state or district test results to identify high-performing students who need additional enrich-

Table 6.4
Teachers' Use of State and District Achievement Test Results for Various Purposes in 2004–2005 and 2005–2006

Purpose	Percentage of Teachers Who Reported Moderate or Extensive Use of Achievement Data for This Purpose	
	Engaged PVAAS Pilot Teachers (n=108)	Comparison Teachers (n=525)
Identify low-performing students who need additional assistance	79	69
Identify high-performing students who need additional enrichment[a]	51	49
Identify and correct gaps in the curriculum and instruction for all students[b]	73	58
Identify areas where I need to strengthen my own content knowledge or teaching skills[a]	64	61
Assign or reassign students to instructional groups[c]	61	47
Set different learning goals for different students[a]	56	45
Improve or increase the involvement of parents in student learning	24	22

NOTES: None of the differences between groups is statistically significant (p < 0.05). Response options were (1) Did not use in this way, (2) Used minimally, (3) Used moderately, and (4) Used extensively.

[a] Due to item nonresponse, n=524 comparison teachers for this item.

[b] Due to item nonresponse, n=107 PVAAS teachers for this item.

[c] Due to item nonresponse, n=522 comparison teachers for this item.

ment. Less than one-quarter of teachers in either group reported using results to improve or increase parent involvement.

Facilitators and Barriers

In this section we present results based on a small number of selected items that address factors that are likely to either facilitate or hinder teachers' use of achievement data. The first question examines the frequency with which teachers meet with school data teams. As was shown in Table 6.3, PVAAS teachers were more likely to report having access to reports provided by a school data team than were comparison teachers. Table 6.5 compares the groups on reports of frequency of meetings with school data teams, and the differences are consistent with those observed on the earlier question about reports: PVAAS teachers were more likely to report having any meetings with a data team, and more likely to report frequent meetings (once a month or more), than were comparison teachers. In addition, we asked teachers to rate the value of these meetings for helping them use data to guide their instruction (results not shown in tables). Among teachers who did participate in meetings with school data teams, 35 percent of comparison teachers reported that these meetings are not valuable for this purpose, compared with only 20 percent of PVAAS teachers. Conversely, 33 percent of PVAAS teachers and 21 percent of comparison teachers described the meetings as very valuable.

In addition to school-based data teams, professional development that is focused on data use is another mechanism that might facilitate effective data-driven decisionmaking. Table 6.6 indicates the percentage of teachers reporting either no professional development or relatively intense professional development (25 hours or more) on several topics related to assessment. The topic that is most relevant to understanding differences between teachers who have access to PVAAS and those who do not is probably the first one, analyzing and interpreting student achievement data, and this is the topic for which the largest group difference was observed, although it is not significant. Nearly a quarter of the comparison teachers reported receiving no professional development on this topic compared to just 11 percent for PVAAS teachers. PVAAS teachers also are more likely to report having 25 or more hours (11 percent versus 6 percent). Responses to the other items are nearly identical for the two groups.

Resources such as professional development are likely to improve teachers' practice only if they lead to improved skills and understanding on the part of teachers. Although we cannot directly measure teacher capacity, we asked teachers their opinions about their own preparedness to interpret and use test results. Table 6.7 shows that engaged PVAAS teachers were sig-

Table 6.5
Frequency of Teachers' Meetings with School Data Teams

Frequency	Percentage of Engaged PVAAS Pilot Teachers (n=108) Who Reported This Frequency	Percentage of Comparison Teachers (n=525) Who Reported This Frequency
Never	24	41
A few times a year	44	45
Once or twice a month	25	11
Once or twice a week	4	2
Daily or almost daily	3	0

NOTE: None of the differences was statistically significant (p < 0.05).

Table 6.6
Teachers' Participation in Professional Development

Type of Professional Development	Percentage of Teachers Who Reported Not Participating in This Type of Development		Percentage of Teacher Who Reported Spending 25 or More Hours on This Type of Development	
	PVAAS Pilot Teachers	Comparison Teachers	Engaged PVAAS Pilot Teachers	Comparison Teachers
Analyzing and interpreting student achievement data[a]	11	23	11	6
Preparing students to take state or district tests[b]	18	20	15	16
Understanding and using the Pennsylvania Academic Standards[c]	16	19	12	11
Understanding and using the Pennsylvania Assessment Anchors[c]	17	16	12	11

NOTE: None of the differences is statistically significant ($p < 0.05$). Missing category is 1–24 hours of professional development.

[a] Due to item nonresponse, n=108 PVAAS teachers and n=526 comparison teachers for this item.

[b] Due to item nonresponse, n=107 PVAAS teachers and n=525 comparison teachers for this item.

[c] Due to item nonresponse, n=107 PVAAS teachers and n=527 comparison teachers for this item.

nificantly more likely than comparison teachers to report feeling moderately or well prepared to interpret results of standardized tests. The difference between groups for preparedness to use test results to make changes in practice is smaller and not significant, but still favors the PVAAS teachers.

Finally, we asked teachers about the extent to which various factors hindered their ability to use achievement data effectively (Table 6.8). Statistically significant differences between groups were observed for two factors, both related to the need for assistance: (1) lack of school or district staff to assist teachers with interpretation of data, and (2) lack of training on the interpretation and use of achievement results. In both cases, comparison teachers were more likely to cite the factor as a hindrance than were PVAAS teachers. Although the other differences are not significant, the direction of the difference is the same for all of them—compari-

Table 6.7
Teachers' Preparedness to Perform Tasks Related to Test Use

Task	Percentage of Teachers Who Reported That They Were Moderately to Very Well Prepared to Perform This Task	
	Engaged PVAAS Pilot Teachers (n=108)	Comparison Teachers (n=528)
Interpret results of standardized tests	**84**	**65**
Use test results to make changes in your practice[a]	84	71

NOTE: Statistically significant differences are indicated by bold typeface ($p < 0.05$). Response options were (1) Not at all prepared, (2) Minimally prepared, (3) Moderately prepared, and (4) Very well prepared.

[a] Due to item nonresponse, n=107 PVAAS teachers for this item.

Table 6.8
Teachers' Views on Whether Various Factors Hinder the Effective Use of State and District Achievement Data

Factor Affecting Data Use	Percentage of Teachers Who Reported That the Factor Moderately or Greatly Hinders Effective Data Use	
	Engaged PVAAS Pilot Teachers (n=107)	Comparison Teachers (n=522)
Lack of access to achievement results for my current students	22	28
Difficult-to-understand reports or displays of achievement results	20	26
Insufficient technological resources (computers, software, high-speed Internet connection)	12	25
Lack of school or district staff to assist teachers with interpretation of data[a]	**14**	**34**
Lack of school or district staff to address technology problems[b,c]	17	35
Lack of training on the interpretation and use of achievement results[d,e]	**20**	**36**
Insufficient time to examine and interpret results carefully[f]	63	67
Lack of flexibility to alter instruction and curriculum pacing when results identify areas that require re-teaching[g]	45	48
Receiving test results late in the year[c]	63	70
Lack of access to information about student growth in achievement[a,c]	32	46

NOTES: Statistically significant differences are indicated by bold typeface (p < 0.05). Response options were (1) Not a hindrance, (2) Slight hindrance, (3) Moderate hindrance, and (4) Great hindrance.

[a] Due to item nonresponse, n=106 for PVAAS teachers for this item.

[b] Due to item nonresponse, n=104 PVAAS teachers for this item.

[c] Due to item nonresponse, n=519 for comparison teachers for this item.

[d] Due to item nonresponse, n=105 PVAAS teachers for this item.

[e] Due to item nonresponse, n n=521 comparison teachers for this item.

[f] Due to item nonresponse, n n=521 comparison teachers for this item.

[g] Due to item nonresponse, n=520 comparison teachers for this item.

son teachers were more likely to cite each as a hindrance. The more commonly cited hindrances were also those that tend to show the smallest group differences; they include insufficient time, lack of flexibility in curriculum, and receiving results late in the year. Interestingly, nearly one-third of PVAAS teachers cited lack of access to information about student growth as a hindrance, even though all of these teachers reported being aware of PVAAS and knew that their schools are participating.

Taken together, the comparisons presented in this section suggest a number of differences in the practices and opinions of engaged PVAAS and the comparison group of non-PVAAS teachers. Compared to their non-PVAAS counterparts, PVAAS teachers described themselves as better prepared to interpret test-score data, reported more access to resources to help them with data use, and used achievement data more extensively to inform a variety of instructional decisions. There are some caveats that should be kept in mind when interpreting these results. In particular, the decision to focus on relatively engaged teachers in the PVAAS districts limits the generalizability of the findings to all PVAAS districts, and may limit the quality of the matching. The comparisons presented so far in this chapter have been based on questions about data and data use in general; the next section provides a more detailed look at how teachers in pilot districts are responding to the specific information they receive from the PVAAS system.

Responses to PVAAS Among Engaged Teachers

As in the previous section, we limit the analysis to teachers engaged in PVAAS—those who reported awareness of PVAAS and who knew that their schools are participating in the pilot program. The first set of items examines teachers' access to resources related to PVAAS and their opinions about the usefulness of each (Table 6.9). Because few teachers reported that these items are very useful, we combine responses of moderately and very useful for these items. Teachers were less likely than principals to report they have access to these resources and, among those who saw them, less likely to rate them as useful (see Table 5.13). In particular, while almost 90 percent of principals reported they had seen the PVAAS overview presentation, only about a third of teachers had. These differences reflect the top-down nature of the PVAAS roll out and may suggest that even though most of these resources are available on the Internet, many principals are not making teachers aware of them or encouraging teachers to refer to them.

Table 6.9
PVAAS-Engaged Teachers' Reporting of the Availability and Usefulness of PVAAS Resources

Resource	Percentage of Engaged Teachers (n=108) Who Saw This Resource	Of Those Who Saw the Resource, the Percentage Who Reported That It Was Moderately or Very Useful
The *Introductory Guide for Pennsylvania Educators* *("Understanding Value-Added Analysis")*	57	53
The *Resource Guide for the Pennsylvania Value-Added Assessment System* prepared by SAS	61	62
The "PVAAS Overview" presentation	35	49
Workshops on PVAAS provided by the district, intermediate unit, or state[a]	46	47
Other information on PVAAS provided on district or PDE Internet sites (not the site where PVAAS scores are reported; i.e., http://evaas.sas.com)	55	38
Other articles, books, or Internet sites related to value-added assessment[b]	63	23

NOTES: Response options were (1) I have not seen or participated in this, (2) Not useful, (3) Minimally useful, (4) Moderately useful, and (5) Very useful. The denominator used to calculate the percentage reporting moderately or very useful was the number of teachers who reported exposure to the resource, that is, who responded with options 2 through 5.

[a] Due to item nonresponse, n=106 for this item.

[b] Due to item nonresponse, n=107 for this item.

Table 6.10 indicates the percentages of teachers who agree or strongly agree with statements about PVAAS, as well as the percentage who mark "don't know." As with principals and superintendents, teachers express mixed opinions on the utility and quality of information from PVAAS and on its effects on their practice. Approximately half of teachers agreed that PVAAS provides an accurate indication of how well the school is improving student achievement, a number that indicates a slightly less enthusiastic response than principals, 78 percent of whom endorsed this item. Notably, one-fifth of teachers marked "don't know" for this item. Moreover, approximately half of the teachers reported that they weren't sure how PVAAS information could be used to guide their instructional practice, and about half reported that they weren't sure how to interpret their school's PVAAS effect. When the teachers marking

Table 6.10
PVAAS-Engaged Teachers' Opinions About PVAAS

Statement	Percentage of Engaged Teachers Who Agreed or Strongly Agreed	Percentage of Engaged Teachers Who Answered "I Don't Know"
PVAAS provides an accurate indication of how well our school is improving student achievement.	56	20
I have made changes to my instruction in response to information from PVAAS.[a]	41	14
PVAAS is discussed frequently during staff planning meetings in this school.[a]	25	9
I am not sure how information from PVAAS can be used to guide my instructional practice.[a]	50	10
PVAAS helps me communicate more effectively with parents about their children's progress than I could without PVAAS.[a]	24	21
I use the PVAAS *projections* when speaking with parents to give them an indication of how well their children are likely to do in the future.[a]	15	17
I am not sure I understand how to interpret my school's PVAAS school effect.[a]	48	13
The information on student growth in PVAAS helps to motivate me because I can see my efforts paying off.[a]	34	23
PVAAS has caused me to increase my focus on low-performing students.[a]	41	18
As a result of PVAAS, teachers are sometimes unfairly blamed for poor instruction that occurred at earlier grades.[b]	49	27
I am confident in my ability to explain conceptually (not necessarily mathematically) how a school's mean predicted score is calculated.[a]	25	22
I focus more on the needs of high-achieving students because of PVAAS than I would without the information from PVAAS.[b]	19	18
PVAAS results are one factor that determines whether schools make adequate yearly progress (AYP) under NCLB.[b]	50	35

NOTES: n=108. Response options were (1) Strongly disagree, (2) Disagree, (3) Agree, (4) Strongly agree (4), and (9) I don't know.
[a] Due to item nonresponse n=107.
[b] Due to item nonresponse n=106.

"don't know" are added to these percentages, solid majorities seem uncertain about how to interpret and use the information. Only 25 percent expressed confidence in their ability to explain how a school's mean predicted score is calculated. Perhaps most interestingly, only 15 percent of teachers correctly understood that PVAAS is not incorporated into a school's AYP determination. Teachers are clearly confused not only about PVAAS but about the state's NCLB-mandated accountability system as well.

Despite a lack of understanding on the part of many teachers, there are clearly some who have used the information from PVAAS. Forty-one percent reported making changes to their instruction and the same percent indicated that they focus more on low-performing students as a result of PVAAS. About a quarter of the teachers reported that PVAAS is discussed frequently during staff meetings, and about a quarter indicated that they use it to communicate with parents. Only about one-fifth of teachers responded that PVAAS had led them to focus more on the needs of high-achieving students, compared with approximately one-third of principals.

It is likely that in order to use PVAAS results effectively, teachers need to have access to the reports in some form. Sixty-two percent of the engaged teachers in our sample responded that they have seen their school's PVAAS reports (result not shown in tables). Of these, 57 percent have seen written copies, and 73 percent have access to the PVAAS Web site. The remaining results in this chapter pertain to the reports and therefore are based on this subset of teachers who reported having seen their school's PVAAS reports. Table 6.11 indicates the

Table 6.11
Engaged Teachers' Reporting of Whether They Saw Various PVAAS Report Components and Whether They Found Them Useful

PVAAS Report Component	Percentage of Engaged Teachers (n=66) Who Reported Seeing the Component	Of Those Who Saw the Component, the Percentage Who Reported That It Was Moderately to Very Useful
School-level reports (table form)[a]	87	44
Graphs showing growth among students in different quintiles (part of the school-level diagnostic reports)	85	51
Graphs showing growth among students in the advanced, proficient, etc., categories (part of the school-level diagnostic reports)	85	56
Subgroup reports (results disaggregated by race/ethnicity, socioeconomic status, etc.)	74	42
Student-level reports of past performance	73	64
Student-level projections of future performance	77	43
Summaries of scores for my own students[a]	62	72
Other custom reports prepared by your school or district staff[a]	47	58
The "hints" feature on the PVAAS reporting Web site	22	66

NOTES: Response options were (1) I have not seen this, (2) Not useful, (3) Minimally useful, (4) Moderately useful, and (5) Very useful. The denominator used to calculate the percentage reporting moderately to very useful is the number of teachers who reported seeing the component, that is, who responded with options 2 through 5.

[a] Due to item nonresponse n=65 for this item.

percentages of teachers who have seen various report components and the percentages of these who have found each component useful for guiding their instruction. Most of the report components have been seen by at least three-quarters of the teachers; exceptions are summaries of scores for their own students, other custom reports prepared by school or district staff, and the "hints" feature. Not surprisingly, score summaries for teachers' own students received the highest usefulness ratings. What is perhaps more surprising is that nearly 40 percent of teachers had not seen these summaries for their own students.

Table 6.12 compares teachers' use of PVAAS reports with their use of other state and district test results. The percentages in the second column are different from those reported in Table 6.4 because Table 6.12 includes only those teachers who saw PVAAS reports, which are a subset of those included in Table 6.4. As with district administrators and principals, only a minority of the engaged teachers reported using PVAAS for any of the activities, whereas a majority reported using other test scores for all tasks except increasing the involvement of parents.

The final set of results presented in this chapter examines opinions on the quality and utility of the PVAAS reports among teachers who saw these reports (Table 6.13). Despite evidence of a lack of understanding of some aspects of PVAAS, discussed above, a majority of teachers agreed that the PVAAS reports are clear and easy to understand. Teachers were more likely than principals (see Table 5.16) to agree that they receive so many reports that it is difficult to figure out which ones to focus on (77 percent of teachers, 51 percent of principals). About a quarter of teachers agreed that the PVAAS proficiency graphs provide essentially the same information as the PSSA reports they receive from the state; this percentage is similar to

Table 6.12
PVAAS-Engaged Teachers' Use of PVAAS Data Versus PSSA Results for Various Purposes

Purpose	Percentage of Engaged Teachers Who Reported Using PVAAS Data Moderately or Extensively for This Purpose	Percentage of Engaged Teachers Who Reported Using PSSA Results Moderately or Extensively for This Purpose
Identify low-performing students who need additional assistance	42	77
Identify high-performing students who need additional enrichment	20	49
Identify and correct gaps in the curriculum and instruction for all students[a]	32	71
Identify areas where I need to strengthen my own content knowledge or teaching skills	39	64
Assign or reassign students to instructional groups	31	59
Set different learning goals for different students	24	54
Improve or increase the involvement of parents in student learning	15	24

NOTES: n=65; only teachers who saw the PVAAS reports are included. Response options were (1) Did not use in this way, (2) Used minimally, (3) Used moderately, and (4) Used extensively.

[a] Due to item nonresponse, n=64 for this item.

Table 6.13
PVAAS-Engaged Teachers' Opinions About PVAAS Reports

Statement	Percentage of Engaged Teachers Who Agreed or Strongly Agreed	Percentage of Engaged Teachers Who Answered "I Don't Know"
The PVAAS reports are clear and easy to understand.	62	8
The information I receive from PVAAS is more useful for instructional planning than the PSSA scores I receive from other sources.	33	15
I receive so many different reports on student achievement that I find it hard to figure out which reports to focus on.	77	0
The PVAAS proficiency graphs in the school-level diagnostic report provide essentially the same information as the PSSA reports we receive from the state.	27	30
Because PVAAS focuses on growth and the state's accountability system focuses on proficiency levels, I sometimes feel like I am forced to meet conflicting goals.	64	17
Our school's performance looks better when evaluated according to growth on PVAAS rather than according to AYP status.	41	37
The PVAAS reports are available early enough in the school year to be useful.	47	30

NOTES: n=65; only teachers who saw the PVAAS reports are included. Response options were (1) Strongly disagree, (2) Disagree, (3) Agree, (4) Strongly agree, and (9) I don't know.

that of principals. Teachers were more likely than principals to express concerns about conflicting goals (64 percent of teachers, 43 percent of principals) and to agree that their school's performance looks better when evaluated according to PVAAS than it does when considering AYP status (41 percent of teachers, 27 percent of principals). About half of teachers responded that the PVAAS reports are available early enough in the year to be useful; another 30 percent reported that they didn't know, even though this result includes only teachers who reported they saw their school's PVAAS report. Together, the results suggest that some teachers have found the PVAAS information clear and useful, but many teachers have trouble making sense of the variety of student achievement information they receive.

Summary

Teachers' responses to the survey indicate that at the time of this data collection, PVAAS had not penetrated into the classroom-level except in a relatively small number of cases. Most teachers had not heard of PVAAS, and among those who had, only about half knew that their schools were involved. If the theory of action is sound, this lack of widespread knowledge of the program on the part of teachers provides one likely explanation for the lack of achievement differences between pilot and comparison districts.

Among the PVAAS teachers who were aware of the program and their school's involvement in it, there was wide variation in use and level of understanding of the information. For example, only a small minority understood that PVAAS is not part of schools' AYP calculations, and only about half expressed confidence in their understanding of the meaning of a school effect or in their ability to use PVAAS information to guide their instruction. Comparisons of attitudes and practices related to data use suggest few differences between these PVAAS teachers and their counterparts in nonparticipating schools, though, as noted earlier, there is some evidence that the PVAAS teachers are more engaged with data use and test preparation in general. Together, the findings reported in this chapter indicate that PVAAS has not yet directly influenced teachers' practices or beliefs in any significant way.

CHAPTER SEVEN

Summary and Implications

The goal of this study was to examine the utility of a value-added assessment system for promoting educational improvement. The primary research question focused on the effects of VAA program participation on student achievement. The study was also designed to improve our understanding about how to use VAA to improve schools. The questions about student achievement effects and educators' practices are related: Both are intended to examine the promise of VAA for promoting improved student outcomes.

The test-score results show no difference in the average performance of students from districts participating in the Pennsylvania Value-Added Assessment System pilot program and students from matched comparison districts. However, the detailed exploration of survey results suggests that these null results may be attributable to implementation problems rather than to the value of the VAA information itself. The survey results also provide evidence of the challenges involved in translating the provision of VAA information into a successful educational intervention.

The key finding from surveys of district administrators, principals, and teachers is that during the time frame of this study, which was prior to statewide implementation, the use of the PVAAS data was relatively limited. In particular, the information was not being used by most teachers, the group most directly responsible for promoting student learning. A minority of the teachers from pilot districts who responded to our survey had ever heard of PVAAS and even fewer actually knew their school was participating or saw the reports. If educators are not using the value-added information for decisionmaking, then we cannot evaluate the quality of that information by observing whether those decisions have good consequences as measured by test scores. Because of the limited impact PVAAS has had on education practice to date, we are unable to draw inferences about the quality of value-added measures from this study.

From a methodological standpoint, this suggests that evaluating value-added measures though their effects on student performance is likely to be challenging if the experience in Pennsylvania holds for other locations. The recent study in Ohio and studies from the United Kingdom suggest that limited usage of the value-added data might be expected, especially when the system is newly implemented. In Ohio, for example, only 14 of 63 districts were considered to be fully implementing the program, though that study provides no information about the intensity of the use of the data. Conducting comparisons that use only those districts or schools that make extensive use the value-added data is also problematic because student achievement in these schools might differ from achievement in other schools for reasons that are unrelated to the use of value-added data, and these differences could confound inferences about the quality of the value-added measures. Clearly, there are significant methodological challenges to conducting the kind of causal analysis this study was designed to support; this type of research may only be feasible in the context of VAA programs that provide intensive assistance to districts and schools to support implementation, and that use a randomized design for determining which districts or schools receive the information.

Implications for Understanding Educators' Use of VAA Data

The findings from this study suggest that promoting effective use is likely to be a key challenge for VAA systems. Many district administrators, principals, and teachers lack experience analyzing and making use of data (Marsh et al., 2006). Consequently, educators do not always use data in the manner envisioned by advocates of data-driven decisionmaking for schools. Moreover, when educators do use data, they turn to other sources. This study found that principals and district administrators are much less likely to use PVAAS data than other district or state data to support their decisions. Teachers rely heavily on the tests they create themselves for information on their students' achievement.

Results from the United Kingdom suggest that greater experience with VAA systems might help overcome the reluctance of educators to use them. Cases studies from the United Kingdom found that initial peripheral awareness of VAA with limited reading of reports and no actions taken in response to the VAA reports gave way to more active use after additional years of experience with the VAA system (Fitz-Gibbon, 1997; Williamson et al., 1992). However, the data from our survey do not corroborate these findings. Among the PVAAS respondents, principals from Cohort 2 were significantly more likely to be engaged in the system than were their counterparts from Cohort 1. There are other differences between cohorts: Cohort 1 schools tend to serve greater proportions of urban, low-income minority students than Cohort 2 schools. Controlling for these factors does reduce the cohort difference and makes it statistically insignificant; however, it is clear that exposure alone will not override all the other sources that may affect engagement and consequently use of the value-added data.

One possible explanation for the difference between the case studies from the UK and the PVAAS results is the accountability of educators to VAA. Saunders (2000) notes that educators are more likely to use value-added data if they feel accountable for those measures. Educators in the PVAAS pilot program were explicitly not being held directly accountable for their PVAAS scores. At the same time, they were accountable for the proficiency of their students on the PSSA, and the status data from this test were widely reported as being used to support many decisions and educational practices. As long as the primary accountability measures involve only proficiency status, teachers' focus on proficiency and information about proficiency may override usage of value-added data. On the other hand, pay-for-performance schemes for educators, which are being used in some states and are likely to involve a growth or value-added component, and other growth based accountability systems, like the Federal NCLB Pilot program, may provide incentives for using VAA data.

Because data analysis is relatively unfamiliar to educators, training on the use of VAA systems is likely to be essential for promoting use of the system. This training is likely to require extensive professional development and assistance from the state in implementing and interpreting the results. This might require a large investment from the state, because educators in nearly all districts and levels will need this training. Investments for teachers will need to be greatest because they are the largest group and tend to be least familiar with data analysis. Given that there is little evidence about the effectiveness of training, it might be prudent to continue to evaluate the training program in a small number of districts before expanding it statewide.

Our review of the training materials for PVAAS during the pilot years and our discussions with the state's program coordinators found that the early training sessions emphasized teaching educators about the merits of growth data and the statistical methodology used by PVAAS. It also provided demonstrations on navigating the PVAAS online reports. However, the training provided very few specific details on using the data for education reform or making specific decisions about students or education practice, and this is precisely the kind of training needed if educators are to make good use of the information. Shortcomings in training could account for low utilization of the PVAAS data.

As the PVAAS program has matured, the training materials have been significantly revised to focus on using data for decisionmaking in schools and on the role that PVAAS can play in informing those decisions. In particular, with the statewide rollout of PVAAS, the training materials now include a two-sided one page "cheat sheet" of questions that each PVAAS report can answer, to which educators can refer as they review the data and plan their improvement activities. The revised training materials have other detailed information to "scaffold" the use of PVAAS data. According to our state contacts, the changes in the materials were made in response to low usage and information that the PVAAS coordinators gathered about the training needs of educators. The state is also focusing on increasing the training at the district level and working closely with district personnel using regional training centers, rather than providing a few large regional or statewide training programs. The state PVAAS coordinators report that the new training materials and procedures are receiving very positive responses from educators. However, the proof remains in showing that educators will make better use of VAA data in future.

Another barrier to the use of PVAAS is the timing of reports and the challenges educators face in combining the PVAAS information with other data. The late release of the PVAAS reports was mentioned extensively as a hindrance to their use in follow-up interviews with a small number of principals and superintendents. Educators also report that it can be challenging to know how to use both the PVAAS and other data when they provide contradictory information. Also, the state PVAAS coordinators report that educators face technical problems in combining data and figures from the PVAAS reports with data from other sources into documents such as school improvement plans. Again, given the importance of PSSA proficiency scores for determining AYP, any factor that might require educators to choose among data sources would surely put PVAAS at a disadvantage and possibly limit its use.

Recent changes in the PVAAS system address some of these concerns. For instance, in 2006 Pennsylvania integrated PVAAS reporting in "Getting Results," the state's school improvement planning framework. PVAAS reporting is also being integrated into other Pennsylvania initiatives such as the Educational Assistance Program (EAP/Tutoring), Supplemental Education Services program (SES), eStrategic Planning, and Response to Intervention (RTI). This integration serves as the intended context to use this growth measure in districts and schools. Also, with the statewide rollout and use of PSSA scores as the basis of the value-added calculations, the PVAAS reports are now available six to eight weeks after the release of the PSSA scores. The state is currently developing a new student identification system, and the implementation of that system should further reduce the time needed to create the PVAAS reports.

Our data indicate that principals who are new to their buildings are less likely to be engaged with PVAAS than principals with longer tenures at their buildings. This finding suggests that repeated training might be required to keep principals aware of the program and using the VAA data. We also found that principals serving greater proportions of minority and low-income students are less likely to be engaged than other principals; in particular principals in schools serving larger proportions of African-American students are less likely to be engaged. Schools with large minority populations are also the schools that tend to face the most significant hurdles under NCLB, particularly with respect to NCLB's subgroup accountability provisions. Therefore, any effort to promote improved data use at these schools must recognize the need to address PSSA proficiency goals simultaneously.

The main findings of this study, therefore, are that PVAAS had not yet influenced student outcomes or educators' practices at the time of our data collection, and that several potential barriers to effective PVAAS use exist. The improved training provided by the state, along with educators' increasing experience in using data and other changes to the program, may lead to greater use in the future. It is therefore worth continuing to monitor educators' responses, although because the program has been rolled out statewide, it is no longer possible to compare PVAAS districts with nonparticipating districts in the state.

Study Limitations

A primary limitation of the study was the small sample sizes for comparing PVAAS and comparison districts. Only 47 PVAAS pilot districts were eligible for our study, 31 in Cohort 1 and 16 in Cohort 2. This made matching districts difficult, especially for Cohort 2. Although the small sample resulted in a larger pool of potential comparison matches, there was less flexibility for making the samples similar on a large number of variables.

The small sample sizes also resulted in limited power for detecting differences in all comparisons. For test-score outcomes, use of student-level data increased statistical power, but even so, for Cohort 2, the standard errors of differences were large and we could not detect small effects. For the educator surveys, the power was very low— especially when analyses were restricted to engaged educators and weighted comparison groups. In these analyses, even large differences of ten or more percentage points were not statistically significant, resulting in ambiguity in the interpretation of the findings. Generally effective sample sizes of about 175 are needed to detect differences of about 15 percentage points for outcomes with base rates of about 50 percent, and sample sizes of about 400 are needed to detect differences of about 10 percentage points. With our full sample we would have had adequate power to detect moderately large effects with our principal sample and moderate effects with our teacher sample.

Another limitation was the possible differences between the PVAAS and comparison districts on unobserved variables. Participation in the pilot required that the school district conduct its own testing in addition to the state's PSSA testing. Information on district testing was not available for every district in the state and was not used in the matching process. We used a large number of variables for matching, with the expectation that they would account for differences in variables that we did not observe for all districts. This might not have been the case. The survey results consistently show that educators from the PVAAS districts are more attuned to testing than the comparison group. These differences might reflect effects of participation in PVAAS, a program that promotes data use. However, given the relatively limited specific use of PVAAS and the tangential relationship between PVAAS and the other testing items, we feel the differences are likely to indicate preexisting, unmeasured differences between the PVAAS and comparison districts.

The potential for these differences to bias test-score outcomes seems limited, because those outcomes are robust to alternative model specifications, including models that control for many student- and district-level variables related to test scores. Moreover, it is not clear that district testing is strongly correlated with PSSA performance, especially after controlling for the other variables we used in matching and our analyses. We cannot test the relationship between district testing and test scores because we do not have data on district testing.

However, differences in district testing histories appear to confound our comparisons of educators' survey results. The general similarities between the groups suggest that PVAAS did not have a major effect on the educators in most of the pilot districts, but caution should be used when interpreting those differences between the groups that were observed.

At the time of our study, the state could not link student scores across time. This lack of individual student growth data prevented us from using growth as an outcome or otherwise using prior achievement as a control variable in our study. To the extent that the districts are well matched (in that students in the pilot and comparisons districts would be expected to have the same level of achievement in the absence of PVAAS), analysis on level scores or growth would show the same results (Rubin, Stuart, and Zanutto, 2004). However, to the extent that there is mismatch between the pilot and comparison districts on individual student growth, controls for students' prior achievement may have been useful.

Although the matched district samples are similar on most of the variables used in matching, the means of some of the district variables for the PVAAS principal and teacher samples do not match means for the comparison groups. The differences between groups might result from the unequal distribution of educators across districts in each sample. Even after various weighting schemes, some differences remain. This is in part due to the small sample size. But it also suggests that achieving good matches at the district level might not necessarily yield similar good matches at the school or teacher level. Hierarchical matching has not been widely considered in the statistics literature on quasi-experimental studies, and our findings suggest it is an area for future research.

The low response rates for principals and teachers also limit our results. The responding and nonresponding teachers and principals were similar on many variables and very similar after weighting for differential response. However, such low response rates increase our suspicions that there are unobserved differences related to the outcomes of interest between the respondents and nonrespondents. Furthermore, if such differences exist, then the bias they introduce will be large with such low response rates. Generally, we would expect that educators most engaged with PVAAS would be more likely to respond to a survey since it would match their interests. Thus, we might conjecture that if low response is biasing our results, it is biasing them toward increased use and involvement with PVAAS. This is, however, only a conjecture and we cannot empirically explore the potential bias.

To capitalize on the quasi-experiment created by the PVAAS rollout, we studied the PVAAS districts in their initial years of the program participation. This design may not have provided enough time for school and district staff to learn to use the data effectively. Also, estimates of school effects can have large year-to-year variability (Kane and Staiger, 2002), possibly necessitating several years of PVAAS reports for educators to obtain accurate assessments of their schools' performances and make the appropriate responses. Moreover, even if the use of PVAAS data is highly effective for students in schools and districts that are exposed to it over time, exposure might not have been sufficient in the PVAAS pilot. Given the complete rollout of PVAAS by the state, we cannot study the longer-term effects of a VAA system with the Pennsylvania data, but future studies of VAA should look for opportunities to study it for longer follow-up periods based on a significant window of time for implementation.

Conclusion

Overall, the study suggests that the primary challenge for VAA systems, like other systems to support data-driven decisionmaking in schools, is to engage educators in using the value-added and growth data supplied by the system. Without engaged use, there is no hope that VAA will affect student achievement, regardless of the quality of the value-added measures. Until use is increased, we cannot fully assess the utility of the value-added information, but instead conclude only that VAA systems have received too little attention to be viewed as effective interventions.

There are reasons to expect that use of the value-added and growth data will increase in the future. Training for VAA systems is changing in ways that are consistent with promoting VAA systems as tools for decisionmaking and providing educators with specific guidance for making those decisions. Use of accountability growth measures are increasing through the pay-for-performance measures promoted by the federal government's Teacher Incentive Fund and the U.S. Department of Education's Growth Model Pilot, and state-supported programs and experience in the United Kingdom suggest that this accountability will increase the attention educators pay to value-added and growth data. More generally, growth data and data-driven decisionmaking are becoming an increasingly common part of the educational landscape, and this should increase educators' appetite for VAA systems and the knowledge needed to make good use of these systems.

APPENDIX
Matching Results Summary Tables and Figures

Table A.1
Cohort 1 Matches

AUN	District	AUN	District
Cohort 1 Districts			
103028703	South Fayette Township	113369003	Warwick SD
103029803	Wilkinsburg Borough SD	113382303	Eastern Lebanon Co SD
104435703	Sharpsville Area SD	113384603	Lebanon SD
105253303	Fairview SD	114060753	Boyertown Area SD
105258503	Northwestern SD	114064003	Kutztown Area SD
106172003	Dubois Area SD	114067002	Reading SD
107655803	Monessen City SD	115221402	Central Dauphin SD
108077503	Spring Cove SD	117089003	Wyalusing Area SD
109426003	Otto-Eldred SD	121390302	Allentown City SD
110141103	Bellefonte Area SD	123461302	Cheltenham Township SD
111312503	Huntingdon Area SD	123465602	Norristown Area SD
112281302	Chambersburg Area SD	125238402	Southeast Delco SD
113362203	Donegal SD	125239652	William Penn SD
113362603	Ephrata Area SD	127041203	Beaver Area SD
113364002	Lancaster SD	127047404	South Side Area SD
113367003	Solanco SD		
Matched Comparison Districts			
118409203	Wyoming Area SD	112671303	Central York SD
115222752	Harrisburg City SD	101264003	Laurel Highlands SD
110171003	Clearfield Area SD	104432903	Grove City Area SD
120484803	Nazareth Area SD	114069103	Wilson SD
115218003	Shippensburg Area SD	112286003	Tuscarora SD
104101252	Butler Area SD	120481002	Bethlehem Area SD
125231232	Chester-Upland SD	124154003	Kennett Consolidated SD
104105003	Mars Area SD	101631703	Canon-McMillan SD
119648903	Western Wayne SD	105252602	Erie City SD
110183602	Keystone Central SD	123466403	Pottstown SD
107657503	Southmoreland SD	115228303	Susquehanna Township SD
115212503	East Pennsboro Area SD	108112502	Greater Johnstown SD
113365303	Pequea Valley SD	107653203	Greensburg Salem SD
113364403	Manheim Central SD	111343603	Juniata County SD
115228003	Steelton-Highspire SD	121394503	Northern Lehigh SD
112679002	York City SD		

NOTE: AUN = administrative unite number.

91

Figure A.1
Histograms of Standardized Bias for Cohort 1 Before (Top) and After (Bottom) Matching

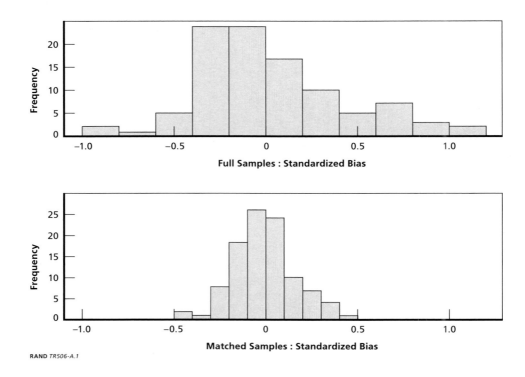

RAND *TR506-A.1*

Table A.2
Median Standardized Bias and Absolute Standardized Bias Before and After Matching for Cohort 1 by Substantive Groupings of Covariates

Covariate Grouping	Standard Bias Before Matching	Standard Bias After Matching	Absolute Standard Bias Before Matching	Absolute Standard Bias After Matching
Population	0.42	0.02	0.42	0.02
Interactions	0.39	0.05	0.39	0.05
Time trend in PSSA score, slope	0.09	0.22	0.18	0.22
2002 district financial data	0.09	0.01	0.19	0.06
2001 racial distribution of students	0.05	−0.04	0.38	0.05
District population 2000 Census	−0.06	0.02	0.18	0.07
PSSA test-score means	−0.21	0.02	0.21	0.07
Average absolute standardized bias			0.22	0.07

Table A.3
Cohort 1 Matches: Balance in Selected Covariates, Before and After Matching

Covariate	Mean in VAA Group	Mean in Full Control Group	Mean in Matched Control Group	Standard Bias Before Matching	Standard Bias After Matching
Propensity score	−1.54	−3.51	−1.86	1.15	0.18
PSSA test-score means					
2001 Grade 5 Math	1,325	1,325	1,314	0.01	0.21
2002 Grade 5 Math	1,331	1,330	1,317	0.01	0.20
1999 Grade 8 Math	1,303	1,312	1,299	−0.11	0.05
2001 Grade 5 Reading	1,322	1,330	1,309	−0.12	0.20
1998 Grade 5 Math	1,311	1,318	1,308	−0.12	0.05
1998 Grade 8 Math	1,296	1,309	1,292	−0.15	0.05
1999 Grade 5 Math	1,307	1,317	1,312	−0.15	−0.08
2001 Grade 11 Math	1,292	1,306	1,281	−0.16	0.13
2001 Grade 8 Math	1,311	1,323	1,305	−0.16	0.08
2002 Grade 8 Math	1,313	1,328	1,312	−0.18	0.02
2002 Grade 5 Reading	1,325	1,337	1,315	−0.19	0.17
2002 Grade 11 Math	1,303	1,319	1,302	−0.19	0.02
2000 Grade 5 Math	1,310	1,323	1,316	−0.19	−0.10
1998 Grade 5 Reading	1,315	1,329	1,310	−0.20	0.08
1998 Grade 11 Math	1,273	1,294	1,280	−0.21	−0.07
1999 Grade 5 Reading	1,315	1,331	1,316	−0.22	−0.01
2000 Grade 8 Math	1,304	1,322	1,305	−0.22	−0.02
2000 Grade 11 Math	1,286	1,305	1,294	−0.24	−0.10
1999 Grade 8 Reading	1,301	1,318	1,291	−0.24	0.15
1998 Grade 11 Reading	1,281	1,298	1,290	−0.25	−0.13
2000 Grade 5 Reading	1,314	1,331	1,316	−0.26	−0.03
2001 Grade 8 Reading	1,304	1,323	1,293	−0.27	0.15
2002 Grade 8 Reading	1,304	1,326	1,295	−0.28	0.10
2000 Grade 8 Reading	1,297	1,319	1,296	−0.28	0.01
2000 Grade 11 Reading	1,279	1,301	1,289	−0.30	−0.14
1999 Grade 11 Math	1,273	1,300	1,279	−0.33	−0.07
1999 Grade 11 Reading	1,276	1,300	1,280	−0.34	−0.05
1998 Grade 8 Reading	1,287	1,313	1,283	−0.35	0.06
2001 Grade 11 Reading	1,278	1,306	1,281	−0.38	−0.04
2002 Grade 11 Reading	1,296	1,326	1,295	−0.43	0.01
Time trend in PSSA score, slope					
Grade 5 Math	5.87	3.27	2.00	0.24	0.36
Grade 11 Math	7.97	5.66	4.68	0.20	0.29
Grade 5 Reading	2.77	1.50	0.39	0.15	0.28
Grade 8 Reading	3.55	3.17	2.65	0.04	0.10
Grade 8 Math	4.13	4.86	4.45	-0.07	−0.03
Grade 11 Reading	3.29	6.08	1.19	-0.22	0.16
2001 racial distribution of students					
Percentage of black students	0.14	0.05	0.15	0.39	−0.02

Table A.3—Cont'd

Covariate	Mean in VAA Group	Mean in Full Control Group	Mean in Matched Control Group	Standard Bias Before Matching	Standard Bias After Matching
Percentage of Hispanic students	0.07	0.02	0.05	0.37	0.15
Percentage of American Indian students	0.00	0.00	0.00	0.06	−0.10
Percentage of Asian students	0.01	0.01	0.01	0.03	0.06
Log(% white)	−0.43	−0.10	−0.39	−0.41	−0.05
Percentage of white students	0.77	0.92	0.79	−0.51	−0.06
2002 percentage of low-income students	30.91	26.50	34.32	0.21	−0.16
2002 attendance rate	94.03	94.45	94.36	−0.23	−0.18
2002 attendance data missing	0.10	0.08	0.16	0.05	−0.21
2002 graduation rate	86.83	90.80	87.75	−0.39	−0.09
District population 2000 Census[a]					
Percentage black	0.09	0.03	0.09	0.41	0.02
Percentage other race	0.05	0.02	0.04	0.37	0.11
Percentage urban	0.69	0.58	0.73	0.35	−0.11
Percentage of unmarried heads of household with children	0.24	0.20	0.25	0.33	−0.06
Percentage of female heads of household with children	0.19	0.15	0.20	0.33	−0.12
Percentage of men with 0–8 years of education	0.07	0.06	0.07	0.28	−0.06
Percentage of men with 9–11 years of education	0.10	0.09	0.10	0.27	−0.04
Percentage of women with 9–11 years of education	0.10	0.09	0.10	0.26	−0.12
Percentage under 18	0.24	0.24	0.24	0.23	0.03
Median real estate tax	1,622	1,535	1,471	0.14	0.24
Percentage of women with 0-8 years of education	0.06	0.06	0.07	0.11	−0.32
Median rent	517	507	498	0.11	0.19
Percentage men not in the labor force	0.31	0.31	0.30	0.03	0.08
Percentage of men with 13–15 years of education	0.20	0.20	0.20	−0.03	0.02
Percentage of women with 16+ years of education	0.18	0.18	0.17	−0.05	0.08
1999 median household income[b]	41,000	41,000	39,000	−0.06	0.21
Percentage of women 13–15 years of education	0.21	0.21	0.21	−0.06	0.10
Percentage with 16+ years of education	0.18	0.19	0.18	−0.08	0.05
Percentage with 13+ years of education	0.39	0.40	0.38	−0.09	0.07
Percentage of women with 12 years of education	0.45	0.46	0.45	−0.09	0.04
Percentage of men with 12 years of education	0.43	0.44	0.43	−0.09	0.00
Percentage of men with 16+ years of education	0.20	0.21	0.19	−0.11	0.03

Table A.3—Cont'd

Covariate	Mean in VAA Group	Mean in Full Control Group	Mean in Matched Control Group	Standard Bias Before Matching	Standard Bias After Matching
Percentage with masters degree	0.04	0.05	0.04	−0.11	0.08
1999 median family income[b]	48,000	49,000	46,000	−0.11	0.14
Median home value	93,252	96,803	94,442	−0.12	−0.04
Percentage not in the labor force	0.37	0.38	0.38	−0.18	−0.04
1999 per capita income[b]	19,000	20,000	19,000	−0.21	0.02
Percentage not work in Pennsylvania	0.04	0.05	0.04	−0.24	−0.02
Percentage over 65	0.15	0.16	0.16	−0.28	−0.07
Percentage of owner-occupied houses	0.71	0.76	0.70	−0.43	0.11
Percentage of vacant houses	0.08	0.10	0.09	−0.44	−0.19
Percentage of women not in the labor force	0.43	0.46	0.44	−0.48	−0.23
Percentage white	0.86	0.95	0.87	−0.49	−0.06
Population					
Population per square mile	2,131	900	1,606	0.43	0.18
Total district population	31,000	20,000	31,000	0.42	0.02
log(population/mile^2)	6.44	5.75	6.43	0.40	0.01
2002 District Financial Data					
log(average daily membership)	2.09	2.05	2.11	0.45	−0.20
Average daily membership (ADM)	4,602	3,034	4,531	0.38	0.02
Percentage of students from families receiving TANF	0.04	0.02	0.04	0.34	0.06
Pupil-teacher ratio	16.26	15.83	16.10	0.25	0.09
Tax effort	22.35	21.15	21.13	0.19	0.19
Transformed tax effort	4.69	4.57	4.56	0.17	0.20
Transformed PITE	3.75	3.72	3.75	0.11	−0.03
Personal income tax effort (PITE)	43.57	42.90	44.18	0.06	−0.05
Transformed average teacher salary	10.80	10.79	10.80	0.05	−0.02
Average teacher salary	49,000	49,000	49,100	0.02	0.01
Ratio of district market value to total personal income (MVPI)	0.55	0.55	0.54	0.01	0.07
Ratio of actual instructional expense to weighted daily membership (AIEWDM)	5,304	5,502	5,251	−0.19	0.05
Transformed AIEWDM	8.56	8.60	8.56	−0.21	0.01
Teacher average years of experience	16.41	16.94	16.86	−0.32	−0.28
Interactions					
Interaction: ADM tax effort	10,5000	65,000	101,000	0.39	0.05
Interaction: ADM, population per square mile	15,822,000	3,724,000	11,250,000	0.39	0.15
Interaction: ADM, MVPI	2,571	1,494	2,526	0.39	0.02
Interaction: ADM, pupil-teacher ratio	76,000	49,000	72,000	0.38	0.06

Table A.3—Cont'd

Covariate	Mean in VAA Group	Mean in Full Control Group	Mean in Matched Control Group	Standard Bias Before Matching	Standard Bias After Matching
Average absolute standardized bias				0.24	0.10

[a] 2000 Census estimates for district population.

[b] 1999 Census Bureau Income Estimates

Table A.4
Cohort 2 Matches

AUN	District	AUN	District
Cohort 2 Districts			
101262903	Frazier SD	112283003	Greencastle-Antrim SD
103026402	Mt. Lebanon SD	113363103	Hempfield SD
103027352	Penn Hills SD	113381303	Cornwall-Lebanon SD
103028302	Shaler Area SD	117083004	Northeast Bradford SD
104432803	Greenville Area SD	117417202	Williamsport Area SD
105254353	Harbor Creek SD	127040503	Aliquippa SD
106167504	North Clarion County SD	127044103	Hopewell Area SD
107657103	Penn-Trafford SD	129546003	Pine Grove Area SD
Matched Comparison Districts			
103027503	Plum Borough SD	111317503	Southern Huntingdon County
104372003	Ellwood City Area SD	117086653	Troy Area SD
104435003	Mercer Area SD	117414003	Jersey Shore Area SD
105252602	Erie City SD	120484903	Northampton Area SD
106160303	Allegheny-Clarion Valley	124159002	West Chester Area SD
106616203	Oil City Area SD	125239603	Wallingford-Swarthmore
108567404	Shanksville-Stonycreek	128323303	Homer-Center SD
108569103	Windber Area SD	129548803	Williams Valley SD

NOTE: AUN = administrative unit number.

Figure A.2
Cohort 2 Histograms of Standardized Biases Before and After Matching

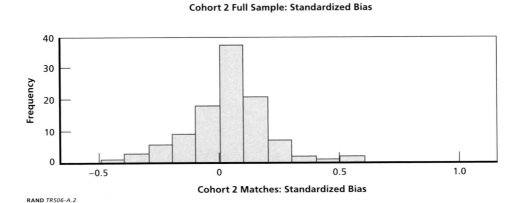

RAND TR506-A.2

Table A.5
Median Standardized Bias and Absolute Standardized Bias Before and After Matching for Cohort 2 by Substantive Groupings of Covariates

Covariate Grouping	Standard Bias Before Matching	Standard Bias After Matching	Absolute Standard Bias Before Matching	Absolute Standard Bias After Matching
Interactions	0.20	−0.04	0.20	0.04
Population	0.19	0.22	0.19	0.22
PSSA test-score means	0.03	0.07	0.07	0.08
District population 2000 Census	−0.02	0.06	0.13	0.15
2003 district financial data	−0.03	0.01	0.20	0.06
Time trend in PSSA score, slope	−0.17	0.03	0.17	0.06
2001 racial distribution of students	−0.19	−0.14	0.20	0.21
Average absolute standardized bias			0.15	0.13

Table A.6
Cohort 2 Matches: Balance in Selected Covariates, Before and After Matching

Covariate	Mean in VAA Group	Mean in Full Control Group	Mean in Matched Control	Standard Bias Before Matching	Standard Bias After Matching
Propensity score	−2.97	−3.51	−3.10	0.84	0.21
PSSA test-score means					
1998 Grade 5 Math	1,333	1,318	1,321	0.24	0.19
1998 Grade 11 Math	1,308	1,294	1,298	0.15	0.11
1998 Grade 8 Math	1,320	1,309	1,304	0.14	0.19
1999 Grade 8 Math	1,323	1,312	1,312	0.14	0.14
2001 Grade 11 Math	1,318	1,306	1,305	0.14	0.15
2003 Grade 11 Math	1,334	1,325	1,331	0.13	0.05
2002 Grade 11 Math	1,330	1,319	1,327	0.12	0.03
2000 Grade 11 Math	1,313	1,305	1,304	0.10	0.12
1998 Grade 5 Reading	1,335	1,329	1,341	0.08	−0.07
1999 Grade 5 Reading	1,336	1,331	1,334	0.07	0.03
2003 Grade 11 Reading	1,338	1,334	1,328	0.07	0.20
1998 Grade 8 Reading	1,318	1,313	1,307	0.06	0.14
2002 Grade 8 Math	1,331	1,328	1,323	0.05	0.11
2003 Grade 8 Math	1,339	1,334	1,326	0.05	0.15
2001 Grade 5 Reading	1,333	1,330	1,325	0.04	0.11
2002 Grade 5 Math	1,334	1,330	1,321	0.04	0.17
2001 Grade 8 Math	1,325	1,323	1,321	0.03	0.05
2003 Grade 5 Reading	1,359	1,357	1,354	0.03	0.07
1999 Grade 11 Math	1,303	1,300	1,297	0.02	0.06
2001 Grade 5 Math	1,326	1,325	1,317	0.01	0.14
1998 Grade 11 Reading	1,298	1,298	1,296	−0.01	0.05
1999 Grade 5 Math	1,316	1,317	1,321	−0.01	−0.08
2000 Grade 5 Reading	1,331	1,331	1,333	0.01	−0.03
2002 Grade 5 Reading	1,336	1,337	1,328	−0.01	0.10
1999 Grade 8 Reading	1,316	1,318	1,318	−0.02	−0.03
2000 Grade 5 Math	1,321	1,323	1,319	−0.02	0.03
2001 Grade 8 Reading	1,321	1,322	1,314	−0.02	0.12
2000 Grade 8 Reading	1,317	1,319	1,313	−0.04	0.06
2003 Grade 5 Math	1,354	1,359	1,352	−0.06	0.02
2001 Grade 11 Reading	1,301	1,306	1,299	−0.07	0.03
2000 Grade 8 Math	1,316	1,322	1,319	−0.09	−0.04
1999 Grade 11 Reading	1,294	1,301	1,295	−0.10	−0.02
2002 Grade 11 Reading	1,318	1,326	1,326	−0.10	−0.10
2002 Grade 8 Reading	1,319	1,326	1,313	−0.11	0.08
2003 Grade 8 Reading	1,345	1,357	1,339	−0.17	0.08
2000 Grade 11 Reading	1,290	1,301	1,289	−0.18	0.02
Time trend in PSSA score, slope					
Grade 11 Reading	8.02	7.38	7.52	0.08	0.06
Grade 11 Math	6.23	6.14	7.34	0.01	−0.11
Grade 8 Math	3.64	5.01	4.11	-0.17	−0.06

Table A.6—Cont'd

Covariate	Mean in VAA Group	Mean in Full Control Group	Mean in Matched Control	Standard Bias Before Matching	Standard Bias After Matching
Grade 5 Reading	3.54	4.49	1.18	−0.17	0.42
Grade 5 Math	4.57	7.06	4.30	−0.28	0.03
Grade 8 Reading	4.27	7.20	4.16	−0.46	0.02
2001 racial distribution of students					
Percentage of black students	0.09	0.05	0.04	0.23	0.28
Percentage of American Indian students	0.00	0.00	0.00	0.17	−0.14
Log(% white)	−0.16	-0.10	−0.07	−0.18	−0.27
Percentage of Hispanic students	0.01	0.02	0.01	−0.19	0.01
Percentage of white students	0.88	0.92	0.94	−0.20	−0.27
Percentage of Asian students	0.01	0.01	0.01	−0.35	−0.13
2002 Percentage of low-income students	25.33	26.60	28.13	−0.07	−0.15
2002 attendance rate	94.46	94.45	94.48	0.01	−0.01
2002 attendance data missing	0	0.08	0.06	−0.08	−0.06
2002 graduation rate	90.38	90.80	90.13	−0.07	0.04
District population 2000 Census[a]					
Percentage of women with 13–15 years of education	0.22	0.21	0.20	0.30	0.55
Percentage of men with 13–15 years of education	0.22	0.20	0.20	0.25	0.30
Percentage black	0.05	0.03	0.02	0.19	0.24
Percentage of owner-occupied houses	0.78	0.76	0.77	0.18	0.07
Percentage urban	0.64	0.58	0.55	0.16	0.25
Percentage over 65	0.17	0.16	0.16	0.13	0.15
Percentage under 18	0.24	0.24	0.24	0.12	0.06
Percentage with 13+ years of education	0.41	0.40	0.39	0.11	0.17
Percentage with masters degree	0.05	0.05	0.05	0.06	0.08
Percentage of female heads of household with children	0.15	0.15	0.14	0.03	0.10
Percentage with 16+ years of education	0.20	0.19	0.19	0.03	0.06
Percentage of women with 12 years of education	0.46	0.46	0.48	0.03	−0.16
Percentage of men with 16+ years of education	0.21	0.21	0.20	0.03	0.09
Percentage of women with 16+ years of education	0.18	0.18	0.18	0.02	0.02
Percentage of men with 12 years of education	0.44	0.44	0.46	0.01	−0.12
Median real estate tax	1,528	1,533	1,399	−0.01	0.18
1999 median household income[b]	41,000	41,000	39,000	−0.02	0.17
1999 median family income[b]	49,000	49,000	47,000	−0.02	0.19
Percentage not working in Pennsylvania	0.05	0.05	0.04	−0.03	0.12

Table A.6—Cont'd

Covariate	Mean in VAA Group	Mean in Full Control Group	Mean in Matched Control	Standard Bias Before Matching	Standard Bias After Matching
Percentage of unmarried heads of household with children	0.20	0.20	0.20	−0.04	−0.04
Percentage of men not in the labor force	0.3	0.31	0.31	−0.09	−0.23
1999 per capita income[b]	20,000	20,000	19,000	−0.11	0.14
Percentage of vacant houses	0.09	0.10	0.12	−0.14	−0.32
Percentage white	0.93	0.95	0.96	−0.14	−0.24
Percentage not in the labor force	0.38	0.38	0.39	−0.15	−0.29
Percentage of women with 9–11 years of education	0.08	0.09	0.08	−0.20	0.01
Percentage of women not in the labor force	0.45	0.46	0.46	−0.21	−0.35
Median home value	90,000	97,000	89,000	−0.26	0.07
Percentage of men with 0–8 years of education	0.05	0.06	0.05	−0.27	−0.06
Percentage of men with 9–11 years of education	0.08	0.09	0.10	−0.33	−0.42
Percentage other race	0.02	0.02	0.02	−0.36	0.03
Median rent	473	506	471	−0.42	0.02
Percentage of women with 0–8 Years of education	0.05	0.06	0.06	−0.48	−0.38
Population					
Log(popn/mile^2)	6.15	5.74	5.41	0.28	0.50
Total district population	23,000	20,000	25,000	0.19	−0.15
Population per square mile	1,128	898	792	0.15	0.22
2003 district financial data					
Ratio of district market value to total personal income (MVPI)	0.59	0.55	0.61	0.28	−0.21
Average daily membership (ADM)	3,500	3,042	3,569	0.21	−0.03
Log(average daily membership)	2.07	2.05	2.04	0.21	0.23
Transformed average teacher salary	10.82	10.81	10.79	0.12	0.39
Percentage of students from families receiving TANF	0.03	0.02	0.03	0.05	-0.04
Average teacher salary	50,000	50,000	49,000	0.04	0.31
Pupil-teacher ratio	15.68	15.69	16.01	−0.01	−0.18
Teacher average years of experience	16.59	16.66	16.59	−0.04	0.00
Transformed tax effort	4.42	4.50	4.39	−0.17	0.05
Tax effort	19.75	20.52	19.62	−0.18	0.03
Transformed AIEWDM	8.60	8.64	8.60	−0.37	0.02
Ratio actual instructional expense to weighted daily membership (AIEWDM)	5,473	5,753	5,486	−0.43	−0.02
Transformed PITE	3.68	3.77	3.67	−0.49	0.07
Personal income tax effort (PITE)	40.27	44.92	40.76	−0.73	−0.08
Interactions					
Interaction: ADM, MVPI	1,885	1,502	1,853	0.35	0.03

Table A.6—Cont'd

Covariate	Mean in VAA Group	Mean in Full Control Group	Mean in Matched Control	Standard Bias Before Matching	Standard Bias After Matching
Interaction: ADM, pupil-teacher ratio	56,000	49,000	58,000	0.20	−0.05
Interaction: ADM, population per square mile	5,367,000	3,723,000	6,873,000	0.19	−0.18
Interaction: ADM tax effort	74,000	64,000	75,000	0.18	−0.02
Average absolute standardized bias				0.15	0.13

[a] 2000 Census estimates for district population.

[b] 1999 Census Bureau income estimates.

Figure A.3
Histograms of Summary Statistics for Absolute Standardized Bias for 5,000 Random Assignments of the 32 Pilot and Matched Comparison Districts

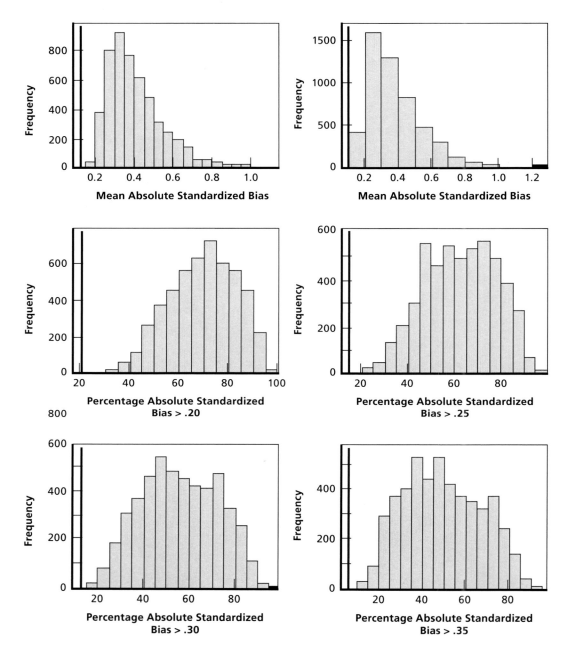

NOTE: The vertical line in each panel is the summary statistic for the actual observed assignments.
RAND *TR506-A.3*

References

Borman, Goeffrey D., Gina M. Hewes, Laura T. Overman, and Shelly Brown, *Comprehensive School Reform and Student Achievement: A Meta-Analysis.* Baltimore, Md.: Center for Research on the Education of Students Placed at Risk, Report No. 59, November 2002. As of August 15, 2007:
http://www.csos.jhu.edu/CRESPAR/techReports/Report59.pdf

Braun, Henry I., *Using Student Progress to Evaluate Teaching: A Primer on Value-Added Models.* Princeton, N.J.: Policy Information Center, Educational Testing Service, 2005. As of August 15, 2007:
http://www.ets.org/Media/Research/pdf/PICVAM.pdf

Center on Education Policy, *From the Capital to the Classroom: Year 4 of the No Child Left Behind Act,* Washington, D.C.: Center on Education Policy, March 2006.

Choppin, Jeffrey, "Data Use in Practice: Examples from the School Level," paper presented at the Annual Conference of the American Educational Research Association, New Orleans, La., April 2002.

Dehejia, Rajeev. H., and Sadek Wahba, "Causal Effects in Nonexperimental Studies: Reevaluating the Evaluation of Training Programs," *Journal of the American Statistical Association*, Vol. 94, No. 448, December 1999, pp. 1053–1062.

———, "Propensity Score Matching Methods for Nonexperimental Causal Studies," *Review of Economics and Statistics*, Vol. 84, No. 1, February 2002, pp. 151–161.

Dembosky, Jacob. W., John F. Pane, Heather Barney, and Rachel Christina, *Data Driven Decisionmaking in Southwestern Pennsylvania School Districts.* Santa Monica, Calif.: RAND Corporation, WR-356-HE/GF, 2006. As of August 15, 2007:
http://www.rand.org/pubs/working_papers/WR326/

Feldman, Jay, and Rosann Tung, "Whole School Reform: How Schools Use the Data-Based Inquiry and Decision Making Process," paper presented at the 82nd Annual Meeting of the American Educational Research Association, Seattle, Wash., April 2001.

Fitz-Gibbon, Carol T., *The Value Added National Project: Final Report. Feasibility Studies for a National System of Value Added Indicators.* London: SCAA, 1997.

Gill, Brian, Laura S. Hamilton, J. R. Lockwood, Julie A. Marsh, Ron Zimmer, Deanna Hill, and Shana Pribesh, *Inspiration, Perspiration, and Time: Operations and Achievement in Edison Schools,* Santa Monica, Calif.: RAND Corporation, MG-531-EDU, 2005. As of August 15, 2007:
http://www.rand.org/pubs/monographs/MG351/

Greenberg, Bernard G., "The Use of Analysis of Covariance and Balancing in Analytical Surveys," *American Journal of Public Health*, Vol. 43, June 1953, pp. 692–699.

Gu, Xing S., and Paul R. Rosenbaum, "Comparison of Multivariate Matching Methods: Structures, Distances, and Algorithms," *Journal of Computational and Graphical Statistics*, Vol. 2, No. 4, December 1993, pp. 405–420.

Hamilton, Laura S., "Assessment as a Policy Tool," *Review of Research in Education*, Vol. 27, No. 1, 2003, pp. 25–68.

Hamilton, Laura S., Brian M. Stecher, Julie A. Marsh, Jennifer Sloan McCombs, Abby Robyn, Jennifer Russell, Scott Naftel, and Heather Barney, *Standards-Based Accountability Under No Child Left Behind: Experiences of Teachers and Administrators in Three States*, Santa Monica, Calif.: RAND Corporation, MG-589-NSF, 2007. As of August 15, 2007:
http://www.rand.org/pubs/monographs/MG589/

Kane, Thomas J., and Douglas. O. Staiger, "The Promise and Pitfalls of Using Imprecise School Accountability Measures," *Journal of Economic Perspectives*, Vol. 16, No. 4, Fall 2002, pp. 91–114.

Koretz, Daniel M., and Laura S. Hamilton, "Testing for Accountability in K-12" in Robert L. Brennan, ed., *Educational Measurement*, 4th ed., Westport, Conn.: Praeger, 2006, pp. 531–578.

Kupermintz, Haggai, "Teacher Effects and Teacher Effectiveness: A Validity Investigation of the Tennessee Value Added Assessment System," *Educational Evaluation and Policy Analysis*, Vol. 25, No. 3, 2003, pp. 287–298.

Lewis, Michael S., and Anirudh V. S. Ruhil, "Achievement Gains Study of SOAR Pilot and Match Districts," The Voinovich Center for Leadership and Public Affairs, Ohio University, Athens, Ohio, 2006.

Little, Roderick J. A., and Donald B. Rubin, *Statistical Analysis with Missing Data*, 2nd ed., Hoboken, N.J.: Wiley, 2002.

Marsh, Julie A., John F. Pane, and Laura S. Hamilton, *Making Sense of Data-Driven Decision Making in Education: Evidence from Recent RAND Research*, Santa Monica, Calif.: RAND Corporation, OP-170-EDU, 2006. As of August 15, 2007:
http://www.rand.org/pubs/occasional_papers/OP170/

McCaffrey, Daniel F., J. R. Lockwood, Daniel Koretz, and Laura S. Hamilton, *Evaluating Value-Added Models for Teacher Accountability*, Santa Monica, Calif.: RAND Corporation, MG-158-EDU, 2004a. As of August 15, 2007:
http://www.rand.org/pubs/monographs/MG158/

McCaffrey, Daniel F., Greg Ridgeway, and Andrew R. Morral, "Propensity Score Estimation with Boosted Regression for Evaluating Causal Effects in Observational Studies," *Psychological Methods*, Vol. 9, No. 4, 2004b, pp. 403–425.

National Center for Education Statistics, *NCES Common Core of Data—Public Elementary/Secondary School Universe Survey: School Year 2003–04, Final Version 1a*, Washington, D.C.: U.S. Department of Education, National Center for Education Statistics, January 2006. As of August 15, 2007:
http://nces.ed.gov/pubsearch/pubsinfo.asp?pubid=2006324

PDE—*see* Pennsylvania Department of Education.

Pennsylvania Department of Education, "Education Names and Addresses," undated Web site. As of August 24, 2007:
http://edna.ed.state.pa.us/

Pennsylvania Training and Technical Assistance Network, homepage, undated. As of September 12, 2007:

http://www.pattan.k12.pa.us/

Raudenbush, Stephen W., "What Are Value-Added Models Estimating and What Does This Imply for Statistical Practice?" *Journal of Educational and Behavioral Statistics*, Vol. 29, No. 1, 2004, pp. 121–129.

Raudenbush, Stephen W., and Anthony. S. Bryk, *Hierarchical Linear Models: Applications and Data Analysis Methods*. Thousand Oaks, Calif.: Sage Publications, 2002.

Reckase, Mark D., "The Real World Is More Complicated Than We Would Like," *Journal of Educational and Behavioral Statistics*, Vol. 29, No. 1, 2004, pp. 117–120.

Robins, James M., and Andrea Rotnitzky, "Semiparametric Efficiency in Multivariate Regression Models with Missing Data," *Journal of the American Statistical Association*, Vol. 90, No. 429, March 1995, pp. 122–129.

Rosenbaum, Paul R., *Observational Studies,* 2nd ed., New York: Springer, 2002.

Rosenbaum, Paul R., and Donald B. Rubin, "The Central Role of the Propensity Score in Observational Studies for Causal Effects," *Biometrika*, Vol. 70, No. 1, 1983, pp. 41–55.

Rubin, Donald B., "Using Propensity Scores to Help Design Observational Studies: Application to the Tobacco Litigation," *Health Services and Outcomes Research Methodology*, Vol. 2, Nos. 3–4, December 2001, pp. 169–188.

Rubin, Donald B., Elizabeth A. Stuart, and Elaine L. Zanutto, "A Potential Outcomes Approach to Value-Added Assessment in Education," *Journal of Educational and Behavioral Statistics*, Vol. 29, No. 1, Spring 2004, pp. 103–116.

Rubin, Donald B., and Neal Thomas, "Combining Propensity Score Matching with Additional Adjustments for Prognostic Covariates," *Journal of the American Statistical Association*, Vol. 95, No. 450, June 2000, pp. 573–585.

Sanders, William L., and Sandra P. Horn, "Research Findings from the Tennessee Value-Added Assessment System (TVAAS) Database: Implications for Educational Evaluation and Research." *Journal of Personnel Evaluation in Education*, Vol. 12, No. 3, September 1998, pp. 247–256.

SAS, *Resource Guide for the Pennsylvania Value-Added Assessment System: 2004 PVAAS Reports*, SAS Institute, Inc.: Cary, N.C.: 2005. As of August 21, 2007:
http://www.pattan.k12.pa.us/files/PAVAAS/PA_Guide_Master.pdf

Saunders, Lesley, "Understanding Schools' Use of 'Value-Added' Data: The Psychology and Sociology of Numbers," *Research Papers in Education*, Vol. 15, No. 3, October 2000, pp. 241–258.

Schafer, Joseph L., *Analysis of Incomplete Multivariate Data by Simulation*, New York: Chapman and Hall, 2002.

Scheerens, J., Cees A. W. Glas, and Sally M. Thomas, *Educational Evaluation, Assessment and Monitoring: A Systemic Approach*. Exton, Pa.: Swets and Zeitlinger, 2003.

Stecher, Brian M., "Consequences of Large-Scale, High-Stakes Testing on School and Classroom Practice" in Laura. S. Hamilton, Brian. M. Stecher, and Stephen. P. Klein, eds., *Making Sense of Test-Based Accountability in Education*, Santa Monica, Calif.: RAND Corporation, MR-1554-EDU, 2002, pp. 79–100. As of August 15, 2007:
http://www.rand.org/pubs/monograph_reports/MR1554/

Supovitz, Jonathan. A., and Valerie Klein, *Mapping a Course for Improved Student Learning: How Innovative Schools Systematically Use Student Performance Data to Guide Improvement*, Philadelphia, Pa: Consortium for Policy Research in Education, University of Pennsylvania Graduate School of Education, November 2003. As of August 15, 2007:
http://www.wallacefoundation.org/ELAN/TR/KnowledgeCategories/ImprovingConditions/UseOfData/MappingaCourseforImprovedStudentLearning.htm

Symonds, Kiley W., *After the Test: How Schools Are Using Data to Close the Achievement Gap*, San Francisco, Calif.: Bay Area School Reform Collaborative, 2003.

Webster, William J, Robert L. Mendro, Timothy H. Orsak, and Dash Weerasinghe, "An Application of Hierarchical Linear Modeling to the Estimation of School and Teacher Effects," paper presented at the Annual Meeting of the American Educational Research Association, San Diego, Calif., April 13–17, 1998.

Williamson, John, P. Tymms, P., and M. Haddow, "ALIS Through the Looking Glass: Changing Perceptions of Performance Indicators," *Educational Management and Administration*, Vol. 20, No. 3, 1992, pp. 179–187.

Wright, S. Paul, William L. Sanders, and June C. Rivers, "Measurement of Academic Growth of Individual Students Toward Variable and Meaningful Academic Standards" in Robert W., Lissitz, ed., *Longitudinal and Value Added Models of Student Performance*, Maple Grove, Minn.: JAM Press, 2006, pp. 385–389.